Fodor's *New* SECOND EDITION
Pocket Rome

Reprinted from Fodor's Italy

Fodor's Travel Publications, Inc.
New York • Toronto • London • Sydney • Auckland

Fodor's Pocket Rome

Editor: Fionn Davenport

Editorial Contributors: Steven Amsterdam, Barbara Walsh Angelillo, Judy Blumenberg, Christina Knight, M. T. Schwartzman (Essential Information)

Creative Director: Fabrizio La Rocca

Associate Art Director: Guido Caroti

Photo Researcher: Jolie Novak

Cartographer: David Lindroth

Cover Photograph: Mauro Sorani/Vision

Text Design: Between the Covers

Copyright

Special Sales

PRINTED IN THE UNITED STATES OF AMERICA

10 9 8 7 6 5 4 3 2 1

CONTENTS

Maps

ON THE ROAD WITH FODOR'S

WE'RE ALWAYS thrilled to get letters from readers, especially one like this:

It took us an hour to decide what book to buy and we now know we picked the best one. Your book was wonderful, easy to follow, very accurate, and good on pointing out eating places, informal as well as formal. When we saw other people using your book, we would look at each other and smile.

Our editors and writers are deeply committed to making every Fodor's guide "the best one"—not only accurate but always charming, brimming with sound recommendations and solid ideas, right on the mark in describing restaurants and hotels, and full of fascinating facts that make you view what you've traveled to see in a rich new light.

About Our Writers

The first time that **Barbara Walsh Angelillo** arrived in Rome, she was traveling on a tight schedule; still, she had time to fall in love with both the city and a dark-eyed Italian—simultaneously. Within a year Barbara said *arrivederci* to her native New York City to settle, marry, and raise three children in Italy. As a freelance travel writer and editor, she loves to share her expertise about Italy with readers, and she has been doing so—mostly covering the regions of Rome, Florence, Tuscany, Liguria, and Piedmont—for Fodor's for more than 30 years. She also is associate editor of the glossy, bimonthly, English-language magazine, *Italy Italy*, which is published in Rome and distributed in the United States and elsewhere.

Editor **Fionn Davenport** has mixed Irish–Italian roots. His love affair with Italy has been a lifelong passion, and from his small apartment on New York's Lower East Side he dreams of owning a rustic cottage on a hill overlooking the sun-warmed vineyards and olive groves of the Tuscan countryside. Art and architecture *do* make Italy beautiful, but he reserves his greatest affections for the Italians themselves: In the words of E.M. Forster, Fionn advises travelers not to "go with that awful idea that Italy's only a museum of antiquities and art. Love and understand the Italians, for the people are more marvelous than the land."

New This Year

A New Design

This year we've reformatted our guides to make them easier to use.

Chapter 1 of *Pocket Rome* includes brand-new recommended itineraries to help you decide what to see in the time you have. You may also notice our fresh graphics, new in 1996. More readable and more helpful than ever? We think so—and we hope you do, too.

On the Web

Also check out Fodor's Web site (http://www.fodors.com), where you'll find travel information on major destinations around the world and an ever-changing array of travel-savvy interactive features.

And in Rome

In 1997 Rome will be in the throes of constructing new viaducts, a new subway line, and various other infrastructural repairs to get ready for the **Jubilee** celebrations in the year 2000. The main inconveniences to visitors will probably be traffic snarls around the Vatican, as construction of an underpass will be underway to eliminate a bottleneck at Castel Sant'Angelo.

Restoration work on the **Colosseum** will continue into 1997, and if Rome's superintendent of monuments has his way, visitors will have to pay to get inside the magnificent arena. He has proposed a prepaid pass for admission to the city's numerous classical attractions; the idea is being considered for nationwide adoption.

Structural renovations of the **Galleria Borghese** in Rome should be largely completed by the beginning of 1997, and it is expected that the refurbished main floor will be fully reopened at that time. This may mean that the temporary entrance, some distance from the main entrance to the estate, may no longer be used.

Also in Rome, it has finally become possible to buy a new pair of socks, or some milk and crackers at 2 AM. Several versions of what the Italians call a "drugstore" opened in Rome in 1996. Actually convenience stores, they are stocked with food and a range of other basic articles; they are the first stores in Italy to open 20 hours a day. One is located in Termini train station and another will soon open in Tiburtina Station. No prescriptions or over-the-counter medicines sold here, though; you can find those at all-night pharmacies (☞ Important Contacts).

The most popular after-dinner drink in 1997 will almost surely be the lemon-flavored liqueur called *limoncello,* available under many brand names in varying degrees of sweetness. Unknown to most until about a year ago, it is now the rage. The best comes from the Capri–Sorrento–Amalfi area, where it was originally made. It should be served ice-cold, and it supposedly aids digestion. In any case, it is delicious.

How to Use This Book

Organization

Up front is the **Essential Information** chapter. Its first section, **Important Contacts**, gives addresses and telephone numbers of organizations and companies that offer destination-related services and detailed information and publications. **Smart Travel Tips**, the second section, gives specific information on how to accomplish what you need to in Rome as well as tips on savvy traveling. Both sections are in alphabetical order by topic.

The Exploring Chapter is subdivided by neighborhood; each subsection recommends a walking or driving tour and lists sights in alphabetical order. Off the Beaten Path sights appear after the places from which they are most easily accessible.

Icons and Symbols

★   Our special recommendations
✕   Restaurant
🏠   Lodging establishment
🐸   Good for kids (rubber duckie)
☞   Sends you to another section of the guide for more information
✉   Address
☎   Telephone number
🕐   Opening and closing times
💰   Admission prices (those we give apply only to adults; substantially reduced fees are almost always available for children, students, and senior citizens)

Numbers in white and black circle—② and ❷, for example—that appear on the maps, in the margins, and within the tours correspond to one another.

Dining and Lodging

The restaurants and lodgings we list are the cream of the crop in each price range. Price charts appear in their respective chapters.

Hotel Facilities

We always list the facilities that are available—but we don't specify whether they cost extra: When pricing accommodations, always ask what's included.

Assume that hotels operate on the **European Plan** (EP, with no meals) unless we note that they use the **Full American Plan** (FAP, with all meals), the **Modified American Plan** (MAP, with breakfast and dinner daily), or the **Continental Plan** (CP, with a Continental breakfast daily).

Restaurant Reservations and Dress Codes

Reservations are always a good idea; we note only when they're essential or when they are not accepted. Book as far ahead as you can, and reconfirm when you get to town. Unless otherwise noted, the restaurants listed are open daily for lunch and dinner. We mention dress only when men are required to wear a jacket or a jacket and tie. Look for an overview of local habits under Packing in Smart Travel Tips.

Credit Cards

The following abbreviations are used: **AE**, American Express; **DC**, Diners Club; **MC**, MasterCard; and **V**, Visa.

Don't Forget to Write

You can use this book in the confidence that all prices and opening times are based on information supplied to us at press time; Fodor's cannot accept responsibility for any errors. Time inevitably brings changes, so always confirm information when it matters—especially if you're making a detour to visit a specific place. In addition, when making reservations be sure to mention if you have a disability or are traveling with children, if you prefer a private bath or a certain type of bed, or if you have specific dietary needs or any other concerns.

Were the restaurants we recommended as described? Did our hotel picks exceed your expectations? Did you find a museum we recommended a waste of time? If you have complaints, we'll look into them and revise our entries when the facts warrant it. If you've discovered a special place that we haven't included, we'll pass the information along to our correspondents and have them check it out. So send your feedback, positive *and* negative, to the *Pocket Rome* editor at Fodor's Travel Publications, 201 East 50th Street, New York, New York 10022—and have a wonderful trip!

Karen Cure

Karen Cure
Editorial Director

Rome

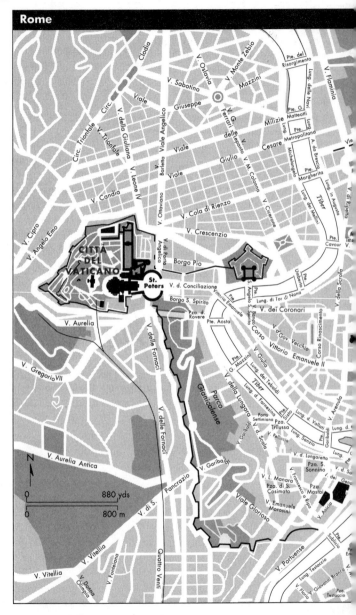

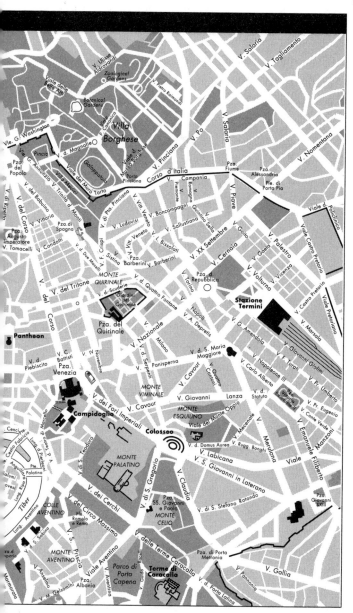

x

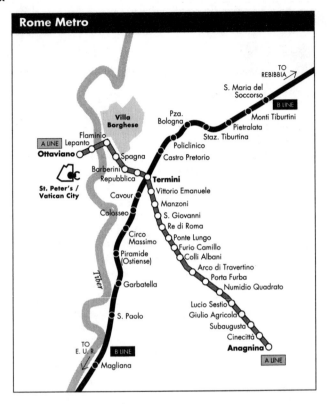

IMPORTANT CONTACTS

An Alphabetical Listing of Publications, Organizations, & Companies that Will Help You Before, During, & After Your Trip

AIR TRAVEL

Most international flights and all domestic flights arrive at **Leonardo da Vinci Airport** (☎ 011–39–6/659–53640; in Rome, 06/659–53640), also known as **Fiumicino,** 30 kilometers (19 miles) outside the city. Some international and charter flights land at **Ciampino** (☎ 06/794941), a civil and military airport on Via Appia Nuova, 15 kilometers (9 miles) from the center of Rome.

Flying time is 8½ hours from New York, 10–11 hours from Chicago, and 12–13 hours from Los Angeles.

CARRIERS

Carriers serving Rome include **Alitalia** (☎ 800/ 223–5730; in Rome 06/65621 or 06/65628246), **Continental** (☎ 800/525–0280), **Delta** (☎ 800/241–4141), **TWA** (☎ 800/892–4141).

FROM THE U.K.➢ Direct service from Heathrow is provided by **Alitalia** (☎ 0171/602–7111; outside London, 0345/ 212–121) and **British Airways** (☎ 0181/897–4000; outside London, 0345/222–111). Flying time to Rome is two hours.

BUS TRAVEL

FROM THE U.K.
Eurolines (✉ 52 Grosvenor Gardens, London SW1W 0AU, ☎ 0171/730–8235 or 0171/730–3499; or contact any National Express agent) runs a weekly bus service to Rome that increases to three times a week between June and September.

CAR RENTAL

Major car-rental companies represented in Rome are **Avis** (☎ 800/331–1084; in Canada, 800/879–2847; in Rome 06/4282–4728), **Budget** (☎ 800/527–0700; in the U.K., 0800/181181; in Rome 06/482–0966), **Hertz** (☎ 800/654–3001; in Canada, 800/263–0600; in the U.K., 0345/555888; in Rome 06/167–808016), and **Eurodollar** (☎ 06/1670–18668 in Rome). **Maggiore** is one of Italy's largest car-rental companies (☎ 06/229–1530 or 06/1678–67067). Rates in Rome begin at $54 a day and $237 a week for an economy car with unlimited mileage. This does not include tax on car rentals, which is 19%.

CONSULATES

U.S. Consulate (⊠ Via Veneto 121, ☎ 06/46741), **Canadian Consulate** (⊠ Via Zara 30, ☎ 06/445981), **U.K. Consulate** (⊠ Via Venti Settembre 80A, ☎ 06/482–5441).

CUSTOMS

IN THE U.S.

The **U.S. Customs Service** (⊠ Box 7407, Washington, DC 20044, ☎ 202/927–6724) can answer questions on duty-free limits and publishes a helpful brochure, **"Know Before You Go."** For information on registering foreign-made articles, call 202/927–0540.

CANADIANS

Contact **Revenue Canada** (⊠ 2265 St. Laurent Blvd. S, Ottawa, Ontario K1G 4K3, ☎ 613/993–0534) for a copy of the free brochure **"I Declare/Je Déclare"** and for details on duty-free limits. For recorded information (within Canada only), call 800/461–9999.

U.K. CITIZENS

HM Customs and Excise (⊠ Dorset House, Stamford St., London SE1 9NG, ☎ 0171/ 202–4227) can answer questions about U.K. customs regulations and publishes a free pamphlet, **"A Guide for Travellers,"** detailing standard procedures and import rules.

DISABILITIES & ACCESSIBILITY

The Italian Government Travel Office (ENIT; ☞ Visitor Information, *below*) can provide a list of accessible hotels and the addresses of Italian associations for travelers with disabilities. For tours *see* Secret Walks under Tours.

DISCOUNTS & DEALS

AIRFARES

For the lowest airfares to Italy, call 800/ FLY–4–LESS.

EMERGENCIES

Important emergency numbers in Rome are 112 for 24-hour access to Carabinieri (military police); 113 for Police (or ☎ 06/4686); 115 for Fire; 116 for the Italian Automobile Club; 118 for medical emergency and ambulance (this number is not yet operational in all areas; alternatively call 113 or 06/5510).

CAR BREAKDOWNS

ACI Emergency Service (⊠ Servizio Soccorso Stradale, Via Solferino 32, 00185 Rome, ☎ 06/44595) offers 24-hour road service. Dial 116 from any phone, 24 hours a day, to reach the nearest ACI service station.

DOCTORS AND DENTISTS

Call your consulate (*see* above) or the private Salvator Mundi Hospital (☎ 06/588961) or Rome American Hospital (☎ 06/22551), which have English-speaking staff, for recommendations.

LATE-NIGHT PHARMACIES

You will find American and British products—or their equivalents—and English-speaking staff at **Farmacia Internazionale Capranica** (⊠ Piazza Capranica 96, ☎ 056/679–4680), **Farmacia Internazionale Barberini** (⊠ Piazza Barberini 49, ☎ 06/482–5456), and **Farmacia Cola di Rienzo** (⊠ Via Cola di Rienzo 213, ☎ 06/324–3130), among others. Most are open 8:30–1, 4–8; some are open all night. Pharmacies take turns opening on Sunday. A schedule is posted in each pharmacy.

ENGLISH-LANGUAGE BOOKSTORES

English-language paperback books and magazines are available at newsstands in the center of Rome, especially on Via Veneto. For all types of books in English, visit the **Economy Book and Video Center** (⊠ Via Torino 136, ☎ 06/474–6877), the **Anglo-American Bookstore** (⊠ Via della Vite 102, ☎ 06/679–5222), the **Lion Bookshop** (⊠ Via del Babuino 181, ☎ 06/322–5837), or, in Trastevere, the **Open Door** (⊠ Via della Lungaretta 25, ☎ 06/589–6478) and the **Corner Bookstore** (⊠ Via del Moro 48, ☎ 06/583–6942).

GAY & LESBIAN TRAVEL

The national gay and lesbian association in Italy is **ARCIGAY** (⊠ Via Acciaresi 7, 00157 Rome, ☎ 06/417–30752), which will provide information on events of interest to gays and lesbians.

HOTELS

If you arrive in Rome without reservations, try one of the following: **HR,** Hotel Reservation service (☎ 06/699–1000), with desks at Leonardo da Vinci Airport (Fiumicino Airport) and Termini Station (an English-speaking operator is available daily 7 AM–10 PM); **EPT** information offices: Via Parigi 5 (☎ 06/4889–9253), Termini Station (☎ 06/487–1270), Leonardo da Vinci Airport (☎ 06/6595–6074); municipal tourist information booths at Largo Goldoni (⊠ Via del Corso), Via dei Fori Imperiali, and Via Nazionale. All can help with accommodations, and there is no charge. Avoid official-looking men who approach tourists at Termini Station: They tout for the less desirable hotels around the train station. **CTS,** a student travel agency, can help find rooms (☞ Students, below).

INSURANCE

IN CANADA

Contact **Mutual of Omaha** (⊠ Travel Division, 500 University Ave., Toronto, Ontario M5G 1V8, ☎ 800/465–0267 (in Canada) or 416/598-4083).

IN THE U.S.

Travel insurance covering baggage, health, and trip cancellation or interruptions is available from **Access America** (⊠ 6600 W. Broad St., Richmond, VA 23230, ☎ 804/285–3300 or 800/334–7525), **Carefree Travel Insurance** (⊠ Box

9366, 100 Garden City Plaza, Garden City, NY 11530, ☎ 516/294−0220 or 800/323−3149), **Near Travel Services** (⌧ Box 1339, Calumet City, IL 60409, ☎ 708/868−6700 or 800/654−6700), **Tele-Trip** (⌧ Mutual of Omaha Plaza, Box 31716, Omaha, NE 68131, ☎ 800/228−9792), **Travel Guard International** (⌧ 1145 Clark St., Stevens Point, WI 54481, ☎ 715/345−0505 or 800/826−1300), **Travel Insured International** (⌧ Box 280568, East Hartford, CT 06128, ☎ 203/528−7663 or 800/243−3174), and **Wallach & Company** (⌧ 107 W. Federal St., Box 480, Middleburg, VA 22117, ☎ 540/687−3166 or 800/237−6615).

IN THE U.K.
The **Association of British Insurers** (⌧ 51 Gresham St., London EC2V 7HQ, England, ☎ 0171/600−3333) gives advice by phone and publishes the free pamphlet **"Holiday Insurance,"** which sets out typical policy provisions and costs.

MONEY MATTERS

ATMS
For specific foreign **Cirrus** locations, call 800/424−7787; for foreign **Plus** locations, consult the Plus directory at your local bank.

CURRENCY EXCHANGE
If your bank doesn't exchange currency, contact **Thomas Cook Currency Services** (☎ 800/287−

7362 for locations). **Ruesch International** (☎ 800/ 424−2923 for locations) can also provide you with foreign banknotes before you leave home and publishes a number of useful brochures, including a "Foreign Currency Guide" and "Foreign Exchange Tips."

WIRING FUNDS
Funds can be wired via **MoneyGram℠** (for locations and information in the U.S. and Canada, ☎ 800/926−9400) or **Western Union** (for agent locations or to send money using MasterCard or Visa, ☎ 800/325−6000; in Canada, 800/321−2923; in the U.K., 0800/833833; or visit the Western Union office at the nearest major post office).

PASSPORTS & VISAS

IN THE U.S.
For fees, documentation requirements, and other information, call the State Department's **Office of Passport Services** information line (☎ 202/647−0518).

CANADIANS
For fees, documentation requirements, and other information, call the Ministry of Foreign Affairs and International Trade's **Passport Office** (☎ 819/994−3500 or 800/567−6868).

U.K. CITIZENS
For fees, documentation requirements, and to request an emergency passport, call the **London Passport Office** (☎ 0990/210410).

SENIOR CITIZENS

Contact the **American Association of Retired Persons** (✉ AARP, 601 E St. NW, Washington, DC 20049, ☎ 202/ 434–2277; annual dues $8 per person or couple). Its Purchase Privilege Program secures discounts for members on lodging, car rentals, and sightseeing.

STUDENTS

DISCOUNTS

Members of **Hostelling International–American Youth Hostels** (✉ 733 15th St. NW, Suite 840, Washington, DC 20005, ☎ 202/ 783–6161 or 800/444–6111 for reservations at selected hostels, FAX 202/783–6171) are eligible for discounts on car rentals. admissions, and other travel expenses.

For similar discounts, get an **International Student Identity Card,** if you're a bona fide student, or the **GO 25: International Youth Travel Card,** if you're not a student but under age 26. Each includes basic travel-accident and illness coverage, plus a toll-free travel hot line. In the United States, either card costs $18; apply through the Council on International Educational Exchange ((✉ mail orders only: CIEE, 205 E. 42nd St., 16th Floor, New York, NY 10017, ☎ 212/ 822–2600, info@ciee. org). In Canada, cards are available for $15 each ($16 by mail) from Travel Cuts (✉ 187 College St., Toronto, Ontario M5T 1P7, ☎ 416/979–2406 or 800/667–2887), and in the United Kingdom for £5 each at student unions and student travel companies.

ORGANIZATIONS

The **Centro Turistico Studentesco** (CTS) is a student and youth travel agency that helps its clients find low-cost accommodations and bargain fares for travel in Rome and elsewhere and also serves as a meeting place for young people of all nations. It is located at Via Genova 16, near the railroad station (☎ 06/467–9271. CTS is also the Rome representative for **EuroTrain International.**

TELEPHONE MATTERS

The country code for Italy is 39. For local access numbers abroad, contact **AT&T** USADirect (☎ 800/874–4000), **MCI** Call USA (☎ 800/444–4444), or **Sprint** Express (☎ 800/793–1153).

TOURS

ORIENTATION TOURS

American Express (☎ 06/67641), **CIT** (☎ 06/47941), **Appian Line** (☎ 06/488–4151), and other operators offer three-hour tours in air-conditioned 60-passenger buses with English-speaking guides. There are four standard itineraries: "Ancient Rome" (including the Roman Forum and Colosseum), "Classic Rome" (including St. Peter's Basilica, Trevi Fountain, and the Janiculum Hill), "Christian Rome" (some major churches and the Catacombs), and "The Vatican Museums and Sistine Chapel." Most cost about 53,000 lire, but the Vatican Museums tour costs about 60,000 lire. American Express tours depart from Piazza di Spagna, and CIT from Piazza della Repubblica, both with some hotel pickups; Appian Line picks you up at your hotel.

American Express and other operators can provide a luxury car for up to three people, a limousine for up to seven, and a minibus for up to nine—all with English-speaking driver—but guide service is extra. Almost all operators offer "Rome by Night" tours, with or without pizza or dinner and entertainment. You can book tours through travel agents.

The **Rome Trolley Tour,** with a recorded tour broadcast, operates continuously on a circle route, making 11 stops along the way at important sights, among them Piazza del Popolo, the Vatican Museums and the catacombs on Via Appia Antica. You can get on and off at will. Tickets cost 26,000 lire and are valid 24 hours. The bus operates daily 9:30–6.

The least-expensive organized sightseeing tour of Rome is run by **ATAC** (☏ 06/469–54444), the municipal bus company. Bus 110 tours leave from Piazza dei Cinquecento, in front of Termini Station, last about three hours, and

cost about 15,000 lire. The driver provides a commentary, and you're given an illustrated guide with additional information. Buy tickets at the ATAC information booth in front of Termini Station; there is at least one tour daily, departing at 2:30 (3:30 in summer).

The least-expensive "tours" of Rome are the routes of certain buses and trams that pass major sights. Time your ride to avoid rush hours. The small electric Bus 119 scoots through the heart of Old Rome, with stops near the Pantheon, the Spanish Steps, and Piazza del Popolo, among other sights. Several buses have long routes crossing Piazza Venezia, heart of the city. They are Bus 56 from Via Po and Via Veneto to Trastevere; Bus 62 from Porta Pia to the Vatican walls; Bus 81 from San Giovanni in Laterano to the Vatican walls; Bus 492 from Tiburtina station to the Vatican walls; Bus 90 from the Baths of Caracalla to Foro Italico. Trams 13 and 19 offer views of many neighborhoods. The fare for 75 minutes of sightseeing is a bargain 1,500 lire.

You can find helpful information, including museum hours and listings of what's going on in Rome in the English language biweekly *Wanted in Rome,* and in the English pages of the weekly *Romac'è,* both available on newsstands. Many hotels distribute the free booklet *"Un Ospite a Roma"* ("A

Guest in Rome"), with selected listings.

PERSONAL GUIDES

You can arrange for a personal guide through **American Express** (☎ 06/67641), **CIT** (☎ 06/47941), or the main **EPT Tourist Information Office** (☎ 06/4889–9253).

SPECIAL-INTEREST

You can make your own arrangements (at no cost) to attend a public papal audience in the Vatican or at the pope's summer residence at Castel Gandolfo. Or you can book through **CIT** (☎ 06/47941), **Appian Line** (✉ Via Barberini 109, ☎ 06/488–4151), or **Carrani Tours** (✉ Via Vittorio Emanuele Orlando 95, ☎ 06/488–0510). These agencies take you by bus to the Vatican for the audience, showing you some sights along the way and returning you to or near your hotel, for about 40,000 lire. The excursion for the pope's noon blessing on summer Sundays at Castel Gandolfo costs about 45,000 lire.

WALKING

Secret Walks (✉ Viale Medaglie d'Oro 127, 00136 Rome, ☎ 06/397–28728) has a repertory of 30 theme walks for small groups conducted in English by connoisseurs of the city who give an insider's view of Rome's major sights as well as its hidden corners. They also offer full-day walks, evening strolls, full-day bike tours, a tour for the physically disabled, and a three-day comprehensive tour of the city that costs about 120,000 lire. Most walks last 2½ hours and cost about 20,000 lire.

If you have a reasonable knowledge of Italian, you can take advantage of the free guided visits and walking tours organized by Rome's cultural associations and the city council for museums and monuments. These usually take place on Sunday mornings. Programs are announced in the daily newspapers.

TRAIN TRAVEL

Termini Station is Rome's main train terminal; the Tiburtina and Ostiense stations serve some long-distance trains, many commuter trains, and the FM1 line to Fiumicino Airport. Some trains for Pisa and Genoa leave Rome from the Trastevere Station. For train information, call 06/4775, 7 AM–10:30 PM.

From the United Kingdom, trains leave from London's Charing Cross and Victoria stations and from Calais. For schedules contact **British Rail** (☎ 0171/834–2345) and **French Railways** (☎ 0891/515–477; calls charged at 49p a minute peak rate, 39p all other times).

TRAVEL AGENCIES

American Express (✉ Piazza di Spagna 38, ☎ 06/67641), **CIT** (✉ Piazza della Repubblica 64, ☎ 06/482–7052). **CTS** (✉ Via

Genova 16, ☎ 06/46791 or 06/467–9271) specializes in youth and budget travel and discount fares.

U.S.

GOVERNMENT TRAVEL BRIEFINGS

The U.S. Department of State's American Citizens Services office (✉ Room 4811, Washington, DC 20520; enclose SASE) issues **Consular Information Sheets** on all foreign countries. These cover issues such as crime, security, political climate, and health risks as well as listing embassy locations, entry requirements, currency regulations, and providing other useful information. For the latest information, stop in at any U.S. passport office, consulate, or embassy; call the interactive hot line (☎ 202/647–5225, FAX 202/647–3000); or, with your PC's modem, tap into the department's computer bulletin board (☎ 202/ 647–9225).

VISITOR INFORMATION

IN ROME

EPT (✉ Via Parigi 5, ☎ 06/4889–9253; ⊙ Mon.–Fri. 8:15–7:15 and Sat. 8:15–1:15); offices also at Termini Station near Track 4 (☎ 06/487–1270) and Leonardo da Vinci Airport (☎ 06/6595–6074). Municipal tourist-information booths are at Largo Goldoni (✉ at the corner of Via Condotti and Via del Corso in the Spanish Steps area), Via dei Fori Imperiali (✉ at the corner of Via Cavour and across the street from the entrance to the Roman Forum), and Via Nazionale (✉ in front of the Palazzo delle Exposizioni). They are open Tuesday–Saturday 10–6, Sunday 10–1. All will help you find a hotel room.

IN THE U.S.

Contact the **Italian Government Travel Office** (✉ ENIT 630 5th Avenue, Suite 1565, New York, NY 10111, ☎ 212/245–4822, FAX 212/586–9249; 500 N. Michigan Avenue, Chicago, IL 60611, ☎ 312/644–0990, FAX 312/644–3019; 12400 Wilshire Boulevard., Suite 550, Los Angeles, CA 90025, ☎ 310/820–0098, FAX 310/820–6357).

IN CANADA

Contact ENIT (✉ 1 Place Ville Marie, Montréal, Québec H3B 3M9, ☎ 514/866–7667).

IN THE U.K.

Contact ENIT (✉ 1 Princes St., London W1R 8AY, ☎ 0171/408–1254).

WEATHER

For current conditions and forecasts, plus the local time and helpful travel tips, call the **Weather Channel Connection** (☎ 900/932–8437; 95¢ per minute) from a Touch-Tone phone.

SMART TRAVEL TIPS

Basic Information on Traveling in Italy & Savvy Tips to Make Your Trip a Breeze

AIR TRAVEL

If time is an issue, **always look for nonstop flights,** which require no change of plane. If possible, **avoid connecting flights,** which stop at least once and can involve a change of plane, even though the flight number remains the same; if the first leg is late, the second waits.

AIRPORT TRANSFERS

If you have rented a **car** at the airport, follow the signs for Rome on the expressway, which links with the Grande Raccordo Anulare (GRA), the beltway around Rome. The direction you take on the GRA depends on where your hotel is, so get directions from the car-rental agency at the airport.

A **taxi** from the airport to the center of town costs about 65,000 lire, including supplements for airport service and luggage, and the ride takes 30–40 minutes, depending on traffic. Private limousines can be hired at booths in the arrivals hall; they charge a little more than taxis but can take more passengers. Ignore gypsy drivers; stick to yellow or white cabs. A booth inside the arrivals hall provides taxi information.

Two **trains** serve downtown Rome from Fiumicino Airport. Inquire at the airport (at EPT or train information counters) as to which takes you closest to your hotel. The nonstop Airport-Termini express (marked FS and run by the state railway) takes you directly to Track 22 at Termini station, Rome's main train station, well served by taxis and the hub of Metro and bus lines. The ride to Termini takes 30 minutes; departures are hourly, beginning at 7:50 AM from the airport, with a final departure at 10:05 PM. Tickets cost 13,000 lire. The other airport train (FM1) runs from the airport to Rome and beyond, with its terminal in Monterotondo, a suburban town to the east. The main stops in Rome are at Trastevere, Ostiense, and Tiburtina stations; at each you can find taxis and bus and/or metro connections to other parts of Rome. This train runs from Fiumicino from 6:15 AM to 12:15 AM, with departures every 20 minutes, a little less frequent in off-hours. The ride to Tiburtina takes 40 minutes. Tickets cost 7,000 lire. For either train you buy your ticket at automatic vending machines (you need Italian currency). There are ticket counters at some stations (✉ Termini Track 22, Trastevere, Tiburtina).

BUSINESS HOURS

Banks are open weekdays 8:30–1:30 and 2:45–3:45.

Most **churches** are open from early morning until noon or 12:30, when they close for two hours or more; they open again in the afternoon, closing about 7 PM or later. Major cathedrals and basilicas, such as St. Peter's, are open all day. Note that sightseeing in churches during religious rites is usually discouraged. Be sure to have a fistful of 100-lire coins handy for the *luce* (light) machines that illuminate the works of art in the perpetual dusk of ecclesiastical interiors. A pair of binoculars will help you get a good look at painted ceilings and domes.

Museum hours vary and may change with the seasons. Many important national museums are closed one day a week, often on Monday. Always check locally.

Most **shops** are open 9:30–1 and 3:30 or 4–7 or 7:30; they close on Sunday and one half-day during the week. Some tourist-oriented shops are open all day, also on Sunday, as are some department stores and supermarkets.

Post offices are open 8–2; central and main district post offices stay open until 8 or 9 PM for some operations. The main post office is open on Sunday 8:30–7.

NATIONAL HOLIDAYS

January 1 (New Year's Day); January 6 (Epiphany); March 30, 31, (Easter Sunday and Monday); April 25 (Liberation Day); May 1 (Labor Day or May Day); August 15 (Assumption of Mary, also known as Ferragosto); November 1 (All Saints' Day); December 8 (Immaculate Conception); December 25, 26 (Christmas Day and Boxing Day).

The feast days of patron saints are also holidays, observed locally. Many businesses and shops may be closed in Rome on June 29 (Sts. Peter and Paul).

CAR RENTAL

INSURANCE

When driving a rented car, you are generally responsible for any damage to or loss of the rental vehicle. Before you rent, **see what coverage you already have** under the terms of your personal auto insurance policy and credit cards.

If you do not have auto insurance or an umbrella insurance policy that covers damage to third parties, purchasing CDW or LDW is highly recommended.

Collision policies that car-rental companies sell for European rentals typically do not cover stolen vehicles. Before purchasing Italy's mandatory theft insurance (which costs $10–$15 a day), find out if your credit card or personal auto insurance will cover the loss.

CHILDREN & TRAVEL

Although Italians love children and are generally very tolerant and patient with them, they provide few amenities for them. In restaurants and trattorias you may find a high chair or a cushion for the child to sit on, but rarely do they offer a children's menu. Order a *mezza porzione* (half-portion) of any dish, or ask the waiter for a *porzione da bambino* (child's portion).

Discounts do exist. Always ask about a *sconto-bambino* (child's discount) before purchasing tickets. Children under six or under a certain height ride free on municipal buses and trams. Children under 18 are admitted free to state-run museums and galleries, and there are similar privileges in many municipal or private museums.

CUSTOMS & DUTIES

IN ITALY

Of goods obtained anywhere outside the EU or goods purchased in a duty-free shop within an EU country, the allowances are: (1) 200 cigarettes or 100 cigarillos or 50 cigars or 250 grams of tobacco; (2) 2 liters of still table wine or 1 liter of spirits over 22% volume or 2 liters of spirits under 22% volume or 2 liters of fortified and sparkling wines; and (3) 50 milliliters of perfume and 250 milliliters of toilet water.

Of goods obtained (duty and tax paid) within another EU country, the allowances are: (1) 800 cigarettes or 400 cigarillos or 400 cigars or 1 kilogram of tobacco; (2) 90 liters of still table wine plus (3) 10 liters of spirits over 22% volume plus 20 liters of spirits under 22% volume plus 60 liters of sparkling wines plus 110 liters of beer.

IN THE U.S.

You may bring home $400 worth of foreign goods duty-free if you've been out of the country for at least 48 hours and haven't already used the $400 allowance, or any part of it, in the past 30 days.

Travelers 21 or older may bring back 1 liter of alcohol duty-free, provided the beverage laws of the state through which they reenter the United States allow it. In addition, regardless of their age, they are allowed 100 non-Cuban cigars and 200 cigarettes. Antiques and works of art more than 100 years old are duty-free.

Duty-free, travelers may mail packages valued at up to $200 to themselves and up to $100 to others, with a limit of one parcel per addressee per day (and no alcohol or tobacco products or perfume valued at more than $5); on the outside, the package should be labeled as being either for personal use or an unsolicited gift, and a list of its contents and their retail value should be attached. Mailed items do not affect your duty-free allowance on your return.

IN CANADA

If you've been out of Canada for at least seven days, you may bring in C$500 worth of goods duty-free. If you've been away for fewer than seven days but for more than 48 hours, the duty-free allowance drops to C$200; if your trip lasts between 24 and 48 hours, the allowance is C$50. You cannot pool allowances with family members. Goods claimed under the C$500 exemption may follow you by mail; those claimed under the lesser exemptions must accompany you.

Alcohol and tobacco products may be included in the seven-day and 48-hour exemptions but not in the 24-hour exemption. If you meet the age requirements of the province or territory through which you reenter Canada, you may bring in, duty-free, 1.14 liters (40 imperial ounces) of wine or liquor or 24 12-ounce cans or bottles of beer or ale. If you are 16 or older, you may bring in, duty-free, 200 cigarettes, 50 cigars or cigarillos, and 400 tobacco sticks or 400 grams of manufactured tobacco. Alcohol and tobacco must accompany you on your return.

An unlimited number of gifts with a value of up to C$60 each may be mailed to Canada duty-free. These do not affect your duty-free allowance on your return. Label the package "Unsolicited Gift—Value Under $60." Alcohol and tobacco are excluded.

IN THE U.K.

If your journey was wholly within European Union (EU) countries, you no longer need to pass through customs when you return to the United Kingdom. If you plan to bring back large quantities of alcohol or tobacco, check in advance on EU limits.

DISABILITIES & ACCESSIBILITY

Italy has only recently begun to provide facilities such as ramps, telephones, and rest rooms for people with disabilities; such things are still the exception, not the rule. Travelers' wheelchairs must be transported free of charge, according to Italian law, but the logistics of getting a wheelchair on and off trains and buses can make this requirement irrelevant. Seats are reserved for people with disabilities on public transportation, but few buses have lifts for wheelchairs. High, narrow steps for boarding trains create additional problems. In many monuments and museums, even in some hotels and restaurants, architectural barriers make it difficult, if not impossible, for those with disabilities to gain access. In Rome, however, St. Peter's, the Sistine Chapel, and the Vatican Museums are all accessible by wheelchair.

Bringing a Seeing Eye dog into Italy requires an import license, a current certificate detailing the dog's inoculations, and a letter from your veterinarian certifying the dog's health. Contact the nearest Italian consulate for particulars.

DISCOUNTS & DEALS

LOOK IN YOUR WALLET

When you **use your credit card to make travel purchases,** you may get free travel-accident insurance, collision damage insurance, medical or legal assistance, depending on the card and bank that issued it. Visa and MasterCard provide one or more of these services, so **get a copy of your card's travel benefits.**

SENIOR CITIZENS & STUDENTS

As a senior-citizen traveler, you may be eligible for special rates, but you should mention your senior-citizen status up front. If you're a student or under 26 you can also get discounts, especially if you have an official ID card (☞ Senior-Citizen Discounts *below, and* Students, *above*).

HEALTH CONCERNS

The Centers for Disease Control and Prevention (CDC) in Atlanta caution that most of Southern Europe is in the "intermediate" range for risk of contacting traveler's diarrhea. Part of this risk may be attributed to an increased consumption of olive oil and wine, which can have a laxative effect on stomachs used to a different diet.

INSURANCE

If you decide to purchase travel insurance, first **review your existing health and homeowner's policies** to find out whether they cover expenses incurred while traveling.

BAGGAGE

Airline liability for baggage is limited to $1,250 per person on domestic flights. On international flights, it amounts to $9.07 per pound or $20 per kilogram for checked baggage (roughly $640 per 70-pound bag) and $400 per passenger for unchecked baggage. Insurance for losses exceeding the terms of your airline ticket can be bought directly from the airline at check-in for about $10 per $1,000 of coverage; note that it excludes a rather extensive list of items, shown on your airline ticket.

LANGUAGE

In Rome you can always find someone who speaks at least a little English, albeit with a heavy accent; remember that the Italian language is pronounced exactly as it is written (many Italians try to speak English as it is written, with disconcerting results). Paying close attention to the Italians' astonishing use of pantomime and expressive gestures will go a long way.

Try to master a few Italian phrases for daily use, and familiarize yourself with the terms you'll need to decipher signs and museum labels. To get the most out of museums, you'll need English-language guidebooks to exhibits; look for them in bookstores and on newsstands, as those sold at the museums are not necessarily the best.

HOTELS

In all hotels there is a rate card inside the door of your room, or inside the closet door; it tells you exactly what you will pay for that particular room (rates in the same hotel may vary according to the location and type of room). On this card, breakfast and any other optionals must be listed separately. Any discrepancy between the basic room rate and that charged on your bill is cause for complaint to the manager and to the local tourist office.

Although, by law, breakfast is supposed to be optional, most hotels quote room rates including breakfast. When you book a room, specifically **ask whether the rate includes breakfast** (*colazione*). You are under no obligation to take breakfast at your hotel, but in practice most hotels expect you to do so. It is encouraging to note that many of the hotels we recommend are offering generous buffet breakfasts instead of simple, even skimpy "continental breakfasts." Remember, if the latter is the case, you can **eat for less at the nearest coffee bar.**

Hotels that we list as ($$) and ($)—moderate to inexpensively priced accommodations—may charge extra for optional air-conditioning. In older hotels the quality of the rooms may be very uneven; if you don't like the room you're given, request another. This applies to noise, too. Front rooms may be larger and have a view, but they also may have a lot of street noise. **If you're a light sleeper, request a quiet room when making reservations.** Specify whether you care about having either a bath or shower, since not all rooms have both.

Rome has no official off-season as far as hotel rates go, though some hotels will reduce rates during the slack season upon request. Always inquire about special rates.

MAIL

Airmail letters (lightweight stationery) to the United States and Canada cost 1,250 lire for the first 19 grams and an additional 400 lire for every additional unit of 20 grams. Airmail postcards cost 1,000 lire if the message is limited to a few words and a signature; otherwise, you pay the letter rate. Airmail letters to the United Kingdom cost 750 lire; postcards, 600 lire. You can buy stamps at tobacconists.

RECEIVING MAIL

Mail service is generally slow; allow up to 10 days for mail from Britain, 15 days from North America. Correspondence can be addressed to you care of the Italian post office. Letters should be addressed to your name, "c/o Ufficio Postale Centrale," followed by "Fermo Posta" on the next line, and Rome (preceded by the postal code) on the next. You can collect it at the central post office by showing your passport or photo-bearing ID and paying a small fee. American Express also has a general-delivery service. There's no charge for cardholders, holders of American Express Traveler's checks, or anyone who booked a vacation with American Express.

MONEY & EXPENSES

The unit of currency in Italy is the lira. There are bills of 100,000, 50,000, 10,000, 5,000, 2,000, and 1,000 lire. Coins are 500, 200, 100, and 50 lire. At press time, the exchange rate was about 1,595 lire to the U.S. dollar, 1,157 lire to the Canadian dollar, and 2,402 lire to the pound sterling.

Italy's prices are in line with those in the rest of Europe, and Rome's costs are comparable to those in other major capitals, such as Paris and London. The days when the country's high-quality attractions came with a comparatively low Mediterranean price tag are long gone. With the cost of labor and social benefits rising and an economy weighed down by the public debt, Italy is therefore not a bargain, but there is an effort to hold the line on hotel and restaurant prices that have become inordinately expensive by U.S. standards.

ATMS
CASH ADVANCES➣ Cirrus, Plus, and many other networks that

connect automated teller machines operate internationally. Chances are that you can **use your bank card, MasterCard, or Visa at ATMs** to withdraw money from an account or get a cash advance. Before leaving home, **check on frequency limits** for withdrawals and cash advances. Also **ask whether your card's PIN must be reprogrammed** for use in Italy. Four-digit numbers are commonly used overseas.

TRANSACTION FEES➣ On credit-card cash advances you are charged interest from the day you receive the money, whether from a teller or an ATM. Although fees charged for ATM transactions may be higher abroad than at home, Cirrus and Plus exchange rates are excellent, because they are based on wholesale rates offered only by major banks.

COSTS
Admission to the Vatican Museums is 15,000 lire; the cheapest seat at Rome's Opera House runs 25,000 lire; a movie ticket is 12,000 lire; a daily English-language newspaper is 2,400 lire.

A Rome taxi ride (1 mile) costs 10,000 lire. An inexpensive hotel room for two, including breakfast, in Rome is about 170,000 lire; an inexpensive Rome dinner is 38,000 lire, and a ½ liter carafe of house wine, 4,000 lire. A simple pasta item on the menu runs about 12,000 lire, a cup of coffee

1,200–1,400 lire, and a Rosticerria lunch, about 14,000 lire. A McDonald's Big Mac is 4,800 lire, and a Coke (standing) at a café is 2,200 lire, and a pint of beer in a pub is 7,000 lire.

EXCHANGING CURRENCY

For the most favorable rates, **change money at banks** (unless the lines are too long; it may not be worth wasting precious time to gain a few hundred lire). You won't do as well at exchange booths in airports or rail and bus stations, in hotels, in restaurants, or in stores. Exchange agencies in Rome may be competitive with the banks.

TAXES

HOTEL➤ The service charge and the 9% IVA, or VAT tax, are included in the rate except in five-star deluxe hotels, where the IVA (13% on luxury hotels) may be a separate item added to the bill at departure.

RESTAURANT➤ A service charge of approximately 15% is added to all restaurant bills; in some cases, the menu may state that the service charge is already included in the menu prices.

VAT➤ Value-added tax (IVA), is 12% on clothing, 19% on luxuries. On most consumer goods, it is already included in the amount shown on the price tag, whereas on services, it may not be.

To get an IVA refund, when you are leaving Italy take the goods and the invoice to the customs office at the airport or other point of departure and have the invoice stamped. (If you return to the United States or Canada directly from Italy, go through the procedure at Italian customs; if your return is, say, via Britain, take the Italian goods and invoice to British customs.) Under Italy's IVA-refund system, a non-EU resident can obtain a refund of tax paid after spending a total of 300,000 lire in one store (before tax—and note that price tags and prices quoted, unless otherwise stated, include IVA). Shop with your passport and ask the store for an invoice itemizing the article(s), price(s), and the amount of tax. Once back home—and within 90 days of the date of purchase—mail the stamped invoice to the store, which will forward the IVA rebate to you. A growing number of stores in Italy (and Europe) are members of the Tax-Free Shopping System, which expedites things by providing an invoice that is actually a Tax-Free Cheque in the amount of the refund. Once stamped, it can be cashed at the Tax-Free Cash refund window at major airports and border crossings.

WIRING MONEY

For a fee of 3%–10%, depending on the amount of the transaction, you can have money sent to you from home through Money-Gram^{SM} or Western Union (☞ Money Matters *in* Important Contacts). The transferred funds and the service fee can be charged to a MasterCard or Visa account.

PACKING FOR ITALY

The weather is considerably milder in Rome than in the north and central United States or Great Britain. In summer, stick with clothing that's as light as possible, although a sweater may be necessary in the cool of the evening. Brief summer afternoon thunderstorms are common, so carry an umbrella. During the winter bring a medium-weight coat and a raincoat. Central heating may not be up to your standards, and interiors can be cold and damp; take wools or flannel rather than sheer fabrics. Bring sturdy shoes for winter, and comfortable walking shoes in any season.

Italians dress well and are not sloppy. They do not usually wear shorts in the city, unless longish Bermudas happen to be in fashion. Men aren't required to wear ties or jackets anywhere, except in some of the grander hotel dining rooms and top-level restaurants, but are expected to look reasonably sharp. Formal wear is the exception rather than the rule at the opera nowadays, though people in expensive seats usually do get dressed up.

Dress codes are strict for visits to churches—especially St. Peter's—and to the Vatican Museums. Women must cover bare shoulders and arms—a shawl will do—but no longer need cover their heads. Shorts are taboo for both men and women. For the huge general papal audiences, no rules of dress apply other than those of common sense. For other types of audience, the Vatican Information Office will give requirements.

ELECTRICITY

To use your U.S.-purchased electric-powered equipment, **bring a converter and an adapter.** The electrical current in Italy is 220 volts, 50 cycles alternating current (AC); wall outlets take plugs with two round prongs.

If your appliances are dual-voltage, you'll need only an adapter. Hotels sometimes have 110-volt outlets for low-wattage appliances near the sink, marked FOR SHAVERS ONLY; don't use them for high-wattage appliances like blow-dryers.

PASSPORTS & VISAS

It is advisable that you **leave one photocopy of your passport's data page** with someone at home and keep another with you, separated from your passport, while traveling. If you lose your passport, promptly call the nearest embassy or consulate and the local police; having the data page information can speed replacement.

IN THE U.S.

All U.S. citizens, even infants, need only a valid passport to enter Italy for stays of up to 90 days. Application forms for both first-time and renewal passports are available at any of the 13 U.S. Passport Agency offices and at some post offices and courthouses. Passports are usually mailed within four weeks; allow five weeks or more in spring and summer.

CANADIANS

You need only a valid passport to enter Italy for stays of up to 90 days. Passport application forms are available at 28 regional passport offices, as well as post offices and travel agencies. Whether for a first or a renewal passport, you must apply in person. Children under 16 may be included on a parent's passport but must have their own to travel alone. Passports are valid for five years and are usually mailed within two to three weeks of application.

U.K. CITIZENS

Citizens of the United Kingdom need only a valid passport to enter Italy for stays of up to 90 days. Applications for new and renewal passports are available from main post offices and at the passport offices in Belfast, Glasgow, Liverpool, London, Newport, and Peterborough. You may apply in person at all passport offices, or by mail to all except the London office. Children under 16 may

travel on an accompanying parent's passport. All passports are valid for 10 years. Allow a month for processing.

PERSONAL SECURITY & COMFORT

A word of caution: Gypsy children, present around sights popular with tourists throughout Europe, are rife in Rome and are adept pickpockets. One modus operandi is to approach a tourist and proffer a piece of cardboard with writing on it. While the unsuspecting victim attempts to read the message *on* it, the Gypsy children's hands are busy *under* it, trying to make off with purses or valuables. If you see such a group (recognizable by their unkempt appearance), do not even allow them near you—they are quick and know more tricks than you do. Also be aware of persons, usually young men, who ride by on motorbikes, grab the shoulder strap of your bag or camera, and step on the gas. Keep your bag well under your arm, especially if you're walking on the street edge of the sidewalk. Don't carry more money than you need, and don't carry your passport unless you need it to exchange money. A useful expression to ward off panhandlers is *"Vai via!"* (Go away!).

The best way to protect yourself against purse snatchers and pickpockets is to wear a money belt. If you carry a bag or camera, make sure it has straps that you can sling across your body bandolier-style. Beware of pickpockets in buses and subways and when making your way through the corridors of crowded trains.

SENIOR-CITIZEN DISCOUNTS

EU citizens over 60 are entitled to free admission to state museums, as well as to many other museums—always ask at the ticket office. Older travelers may be eligible for special fares on Alitalia. When renting a car, **ask about promotional car-rental discounts**—they can net lower costs than your senior-citizen discount.

To qualify for age-related discounts, **mention your senior-citizen status up front** when booking hotel reservations, not when checking out, and before you're seated in restaurants, not when paying the bill. Note that discounts may be limited to certain menus, days, or hours. When renting a car, **ask about promotional car-rental discounts**—they can net even lower costs than your senior-citizen discount.

TELEPHONES

LONG-DISTANCE

Since hotels tend to overcharge, sometimes exorbitantly, for long-distance and international calls, it is best to make such calls from Telefoni offices, where operators will assign you a booth, help you place your call, and collect payment when you have finished, at no extra charge. There are Telefoni offices, designated TELECOM), in all cities and towns, usually in major train stations and in the center business districts. **You can make collect calls from any phone by dialing 172-1011, which will get you an English-speaking operator.** Rates to the United States are lowest round the clock on Sunday and 11 PM–8 AM, Italian time, on weekdays.

You can place a direct call to the United States by reversing the charges or using your phone credit card number. When calling from pay telephones, insert a 200-lire coin (which will be returned upon completion of your call). You automatically reach an operator in the country of destination and thereby avoid all language difficulties.

A call from the United States to Rome would be dialed as follows: 011 + 39 + 6 + phone number.

PAY PHONES

Pay phones take either a 200-lire coin, two 100-lire coins, a 500-lire coin, or a *carta telefonica* (prepaid calling card). Scheda phones are becoming common everywhere. You buy the card (values vary—5,000 lire, 10,000 lire, etc.) at Telefoni offices, post offices, and tobacconists. Tear off the corner of the card, and insert it in the slot. When you dial, its value appears in the window. After you hang up, the card is returned so you can use it until its value runs out.

TIPPING

The following guidelines apply in Rome, but Italians tip smaller amounts in smaller cities and towns. Tips may not be expected in cafés and taxis north of Rome.

In restaurants a service charge of about 15% usually appears as a separate item on your check. A few restaurants state on the menu that cover and service charge are included. Either way, it's customary to leave an additional 5%–10% tip for the waiter, depending on the service. Tip checkroom attendants 500 lire per person, rest room attendants 200 lire; in both cases tip more in expensive hotels and restaurants. Tip 100 lire for whatever you drink standing up at a coffee bar, 500 lire or more for table service in a smart café, and less in neighborhood cafés. At a hotel bar tip 1,000 lire and up for a round or two of cocktails.

Taxi drivers are usually happy with 5%–10% of the meter amount. Railway and airport porters charge a fixed rate per bag. Tip an additional 500 lire per person, but more if the porter is very helpful. Theater ushers expect 500 lire per person, but more for very expensive seats. Give a barber 2,000–3,000 lire and a hairdresser's assistant 3,000–8,000 lire for a shampoo or cut, depending on the type of establishment.

On sightseeing tours, tip guides about 2,000 lire per person for a half-day group tour, more if they are very good. In museums and other places of interest where admission is free, a contribution is expected; give anything from 500 to 1,000 lire for one or two persons, more if the guardian has been especially helpful. Service station attendants are tipped only for special services.

In hotels, give the *portiere* (concierge) about 15% of his bill for services, or 5,000–10,000 lire if he has been generally helpful. For two people in a double room, leave the chambermaid about 1,000 lire per day, or about 4,000–5,000 a week, in a moderately priced hotel; tip a minimum of 1,000 lire for valet or room service. Increase these amounts by one-half in an expensive hotel, and double them in a very expensive hotel. In very expensive hotels, tip doormen 1,000 lire for calling a cab and 2,000 lire for carrying bags to the check-in desk, bellhops 3,000–5,000 lire for carrying your bags to the room and 3,000–5,000 lire for room service. One-third to one-half of these amounts is acceptable in moderately priced hotels.

TRANSPORTATION

Although most of Rome's sights are in a relatively circumscribed area, the city is too large to be seen solely on foot. Take the Metro (subway), a bus, or a taxi to the area you plan to visit, and expect to do a lot of walking once you're there. Wear a pair of comfortable, sturdy shoes, preferably with rubber or crepe soles to cushion the impact of the *sampietrini* (cobblestones). Heed our advice on security and get away from the noise and polluted air of heavily trafficked streets by taking parallel streets whenever possible. You can buy transportation-route maps at newsstands, and ATAC (Rome's public transit authority) information and ticket booths may have free maps, which can also be obtained from the municipal information booths. The free city map distributed by Rome EPT offices is good; it also shows Metro and bus routes, although bus routes are not always marked clearly.

Rome's integrated **Metrebus** transportation system includes buses and trams (ATAC), Metro and suburban trains and buses (CO-TRAL), and some other suburban trains (FS) run by the state railways. A ticket valid for 75 minutes on any combination of buses and trams and one entrance to the Metro costs 1,500 lire. You are supposed to date-stamp your ticket when you board the first vehicle, stamping it again when boarding for the last time within 75 minutes. Tickets are sold at tobacconists, newsstands, some coffee bars, automatic ticket machines positioned in Metro stations and some bus stops, and at ATAC and ACOTRAL ticket booths (in some Metro stations, on the lower concourse at Termini station, and at a few main bus terminals). A BIG tourist ticket, valid for one day on all public transport, costs 6,000 lire. A weekly ticket (Settimanale, also known as CIS) costs 24,000 lire and can be purchased only at ATAC booths. Try to avoid the rush hours (8–9, 1–2:30, 7–8), and beware of pickpockets, especially when boarding and getting off vehicles, particularly on the Metro and on Buses 64 (Termini–Vatican) and 218 and 660 (Catacombs). When purchasing tickets for excursions outside Rome on COTRAL buses or trains, buy a return ticket, too, to save time at the other end.

BUS

Orange ATAC city buses and tram lines run from about 6 AM to about midnight, with night buses (indicated N) on some lines. *Remember to board at the back and exit at the middle.* The compact electric buses of Line 119 take a handy route through the center of Rome that can save lots of steps. For ATAC information call 06/469–54444.

HORSE-DRAWN CARRIAGE

A ride in a horse-drawn carriage can be fun when traffic is light, especially on a Sunday or holiday or during the summer. Come to terms with the driver before starting out. City-regulated rates are about 50,000 lire for a 30-minute ride, and about 85,000 for an hour. Refuse to pay more. You can find carriages at Piazza di Spagna, Piazza Venezia and on Via del Corso near the Hotel Plaza.

METRO

This is the easiest and fastest way to get around and there are stops near most of the main tourist attractions. The Metro opens at 5:30 AM, and the last trains leave the farthest station at 11:30 PM. There are two lines—A and B—which intersect at Termini Station.

SCOOTER

You can rent a moped or scooter and mandatory helmet at **Scoot-a-Long** (⊠ Via Cavour 302, ☎ 06/678–0206), **St. Peter's Moto** (⊠ Via di Porta Castello 43, ☎ 06/687–5714), or **Happy Rent** (⊠ Piazza Esquilino 8/h, ☎ 06/481–8185).

TAXI

Taxis in Rome do not cruise, but if empty they will stop if you flag them down. Taxis wait at stands and can also be called by phone, in which case you're charged a small supplement. The meter starts at 6,400 lire, a fixed rate for the first 3 kilometers (2 miles); there are supplements for night service (10 PM–7 AM) and on Sundays and holidays, as well as for each piece of baggage. Avoid unmarked, unauthorized, unmetered gypsy cabs (numerous at airports and train stations), whose drivers actively solicit your trade and may demand astronomical fares. Use only licensed, metered yellow or white cabs, identified by a numbered shield on the side, an illuminated taxi sign on the roof, and a plaque next to the license plate reading SERVIZIO PUBBLICO. To call a cab, dial 3875, 3570, 4994, or 88177. **Radio Taxi** (☎ 06/3875) accepts American Express and Diners Club credit cards, but you must specify when calling that you will pay that way.

VISITOR INFORMATION

You can find helpful information, including museum hours and listings of what's going on in Rome in the English language biweekly *Wanted in Rome,* and in the English pages of the weekly *Romac'è,* both available on newsstands. Many hotels distribute the free booklet *"Un Ospite a Roma"* ("A Guest in Rome"), with selected listings.

WHEN TO GO

The main tourist season runs from April to mid-October. It follows that for serious sightseers the best months are from fall to early spring. The so-called low season may be cooler and inevitably rainier, but it has its rewards: less time waiting on lines and closer-up, unhurried views of what you want to see. Weatherwise, the best months for sightseeing are April, May, June, September, and October, generally pleasant and not too hot. The hottest months are July and August, when brief afternoon

It helps to be pushy in airports.

Introducing the revolutionary new TransPorter™ from American Tourister®. It's the first suitcase you can push around without a fight. TransPorter's™ exclusive four-wheel design lets you push it in front of you with almost no effort–the wheels take the weight. Or pull it on two wheels if you choose. You can even stack on other bags and use it like a luggage cart.

Stable 4-wheel design.

TransPorter™ is designed like a dresser, with built-in shelves to organize your belongings. Or collapse the shelves and pack it like a traditional suitcase. Inside, there's a suiter feature to help keep suits and dresses from wrinkling. When push comes to shove, you can't beat a TransPorter.™ For more information on how you can be this pushy, call 1-800-542-1300.

Shelves collapse on command.

thunderstorms are common. Winters are relatively mild but always include some rainy spells.

Foreign tourists crowd the city at Easter, when Italians flock to resorts and to the country. From March through May, bus loads of eager schoolchildren on excursions take artistic and historical sites by storm.

If you can avoid it, don't travel at all in Italy in August, when much of the population is on the move, especially around Ferragosto, the August 15 national holiday, when Rome is deserted and many restaurants and shops are closed. (Of course, with residents away on vacation, this makes crowds less of a bother for tourists.)

CLIMATE

The following are average daily maximum and minimum temperatures for Rome.

CLIMATE IN ROME

Jan.	52F	11C	May	74F	23C	Sept.	79F	26C
	40	5		56	13		62	17
Feb.	55F	13C	June	82F	28C	Oct.	71F	22C
	42	6		63	17		55	13
Mar.	59F	15C	July	87F	30C	Nov.	61F	16C
	45	7		67	20		49	10
Apr.	66F	19C	Aug.	86F	30C	Dec.	55F	13C
	50	10		67	20		44	6

1 Destination: Rome

The city to which all roads lead, Mamma Roma enthralls visitors today as she has since time immemorial. Here is where Nero fiddled, where Mark Antony praised Caesar, and where Charlemagne was crowned—and the wonder is that you can walk precisely where these events occurred. Hallowed by golden light and thick with treasures, Rome has more masterpieces per square foot than any other place on earth. Nowhere else will you find such a heady mix of eternity, elegance, earthiness, and energy.

THE ETERNAL CITY

Updated by Barbara Walsh Angelillo

COMING OFF the autostrada at Roma Nord or Roma Sud, you can tell by the traffic that you are entering a grand nexus: All roads lead to Rome. And then the interminable suburbs, the railroad crossings, the intersections—no wonder they call it the Eternal City. As you enter the city proper, features that match your expectations begin to take shape: a bridge with heroic statues along its parapets; a towering cake of frothy marble decorated with allegorical figures in extravagant poses; a piazza and an obelisk under an umbrella of pine trees. Then you spot what looks like a multistory parking lot; with a gasp, you realize it is the fabled Colosseum.

The excitement of arriving in Rome jolts the senses and sharpens expectations. More than Florence, more than Venice, Rome is Italy's treasure storehouse, packed as it is with masterpieces from more than two millennia of artistic achievement. Here, the ancient Romans made us heirs-in-law to what we call Western civilization; here, Michelangelo painted the Sistine Ceiling; here, at Cinecittà Studios, Federico Fellini filmed *La Dolce Vita* and *8½*. Little wonder that for centuries Rome has been

challenging visitors to produce a better superlative than "the greatest," a term travelers who become intimate with the city find totally inadequate.

History is ever present here, knit into the fabric of everyday life. Popes, Vandals, the Borgias and Napoléon, Gianlorenzo Bernini, Mussolini, and the ancient Romans themselves all left their physical and spiritual marks on the city. Students walk dogs in the park that used to be the mausoleum of the family of the Emperor Augustus; Raphaelesque madonnas line up for buses on every corner. Modern Rome has one foot in the past, one in the present—a delightful stance that allows you to have coffee in a square designed by Bernini, then take a subway home to a flat in a renovated Renaissance palace. "When you first come here you assume that you must burrow about in ruins and prowl in museums to get back to the days of Numa Pompilius or Mark Anthony," Maud Howe observes in her book, *Roma Beata*. "It is not necessary; you only have to live, and the common happenings of daily life— yes, even the trolley car and your bicycle—carry you back in turn to the Dark Ages, to the early Christians, even to prehistoric Rome."

Rome is often regarded by tourists as merely an introduction or a farewell: They arrive at Rome's airport, stay a night or two, then depart for a tour of Italy. But there are too many Romes—Early Christian, Ancient, Baroque, Etruscan, Neoclassical, Papal—to treat the city as just a jumping-off point. Whether your Roman visit turns out to be a short or long one, keep your sightseeing schedule flexible. Plan your day to take into account the wide diversity of opening times—which usually means mixing classical and Baroque, museums and parks, the center and the environs. No one will fault you for choosing a lazy ramble through a picturesque quarter of Old Rome over a deadly earnest trek through marbled miles of museum corridors.

Remember, *"Bisogna vivere a Roma coi costumi di Roma"* (When in Rome, do as Rome does). Don't feel intimidated by the press of art and culture. Instead, contemplate the grandeur from a table at a sun-drenched café on Piazza Navona; let Rome's colorful life flow around you without feeling guilty because you haven't seen everything. It can't be done, anyway. There's just so much here that you will have to come back again, so be sure to throw a coin in the Trevi Fountain. It works.

Pleasures and Pastimes

The Art of Enjoying Art

Travel veterans will tell you that the endless series of masterpieces in Rome's churches, palaces, and museums can cause first-time visitors—eyes glazed over from a heavy downpour of images, dates, and names—to lean, Pisa-like, on their companions for support. The secret, of course, is to act like a turtle—not a hare—and take your sweet time. Instead of trotting after briskly efficient tour guides, allow the splendors of the age to unfold—slowly. Get out and explore the actual settings—medieval chapels, Rococo palaces—for which these marvelous examples of Italy's art and sculpture were conceived centuries ago and where many of them may still be seen in situ.

Museums are only the most obvious places to view art; there are always the trompe l'oeil renderings of Assumptions that float across Baroque church ceilings and piazza scenes that might be Renaissance paintings brought to life. You'll find that after three days traipsing through museums, a walk through a quiet neighborhood will act as a much-needed restorative of perspective.

Dining

Eating is the Romans' main preoccupation, aside from their families and perhaps their cars. Dining out is all the nightlife most

Romans need, and a summer evening's meal alfresco can be one of the city's most pleasant experiences. There was a time when you could predict the clientele and prices of a Roman eating establishment by whether it was called a *ristorante* (restaurant), a trattoria, or an *osteria* (tavern). Now these names are interchangeable. A rustic-looking spot that calls itself an osteria may turn out to be chic and expensive. Generally speaking, however, a trattoria is a family-run place, simpler in decor, menu, and service—and slightly less expensive—than a ristorante. A true osteria is a wineshop, very basic and down-to-earth, where the only function of the food is to keep the customers sober.

Festivals and Seasonal Events

DEC.–JUNE➤ The **Opera Season** is in full swing.

JAN. 5–6➤ **Epiphany Celebrations.** Roman Catholic Epiphany Fair at Piazza Navona.

MAR. 28➤ A torchlit nighttime **Good Friday Procession** led by the pope winds from the Colosseum past the Forum and up the Palatine Hill.

SUMMER➤ The Summer **Flower Festival,** in Genzano (Rome), is a religious procession along streets carpeted with flowers in magnificent designs.

DEC. 31➤ Rome stages a rousing **New Year's Eve** celebration, with fireworks, in Piazza del Popolo.

Lodging

Rome has the range of accommodations you would expect of any great city, from the squalid *pensioni* (boardinghouses) around the railway station to the grand monuments to luxury and elegance on Via Vittorio Veneto. Appearances can be misleading here: many crumbling stucco facades may promise little from the outside, but they often hide interiors of considerable elegance.

Great Itineraries
IF YOU HAVE 3 DAYS

Begin your first day at Piazza Venezia and see the Capitoline Hill, the Roman Forum, Palatine Hill and Colosseum to get an idea of "The Grandeur that was Rome." In the afternoon, visit St. Peter's and the Sistine Chapel. The following morning, walk through Baroque Rome to see jewel-encrusted churches such as the Gesù, Caravaggio paintings in Santa Maria del Popolo and San Luigi dei Francesci, and urban showstoppers such as Piazza Navona and the Pantheon, one of the world's most beautiful buildings. After lunch, combine sightseeing with shopping and make your way through the picture-postcard neighborhood around the Spanish Steps and Trevi Fountain. Your third morning should be devoted to spending some time in one of the museums that interest you the most and then relax at a café and watch the passing parade until it is time for lunch. Spend your final afternoon and evening exploring the picturesque Ghetto and Trastevere neighborhoods.

IF YOU HAVE 5 DAYS

If you have an extra couple of days, spend your first three exploring the sights covered above, but on the morning of the fourth day wander through Villa Borghese and see the Canova and Bernini sculptures in the Galleria Borghese. On the fifth day, make an excursion either to the Appian Way or to Ostia Antica, an ancient city comparable to Pompeii for interest and atmosphere. In the afternoon, see some of Rome's most historic churches and Michelangelo's *Moses*.

IF YOU HAVE 7 DAYS

Devote more time to the museums and galleries mentioned above that interest you most. Explore one of the neighborhoods you liked best, allowing plenty of time for poking into odd corners and courtyards and churches, and for café-sitting. Make a couple of excursions outside Rome.

2 Exploring Rome

WITH MORE MASTERPIECES per square foot than any other city in the world, Rome presents a particular challenge for visitors: Just as they begin to feel hopelessly smitten by the spell of the city, they realize they don't have the time—let alone the stamina—to see more than a fraction of its treasures. It's wise to start out knowing this, and to have a focused itinerary. These 10 tours of clustered sightseeing encapsulate quintessential Rome while allowing roamers to make minidiscoveries of their own not found in the guidebooks.

We begin where Rome itself began—amid the ancient ruins of the Roman Forum—and then follow up with a look at St. Peter's and the Vatican. Combined with strolls around central Rome—the *centro storico* (historic center) and its indescribably sumptuous Baroque artworks—these itineraries introduce you to the sights highest on practically everyone's list of priorities. The first itinerary is an introduction to "The grandeur that was Rome": the Capitoline Hill, the Roman Forum, and the Colosseum. The second and third itineraries take you through the incomparable sights of St. Peter's Basilica, the Sistine Chapel, and the Vatican Museums. Next we cover Baroque Rome—jewel-encrusted churches, Caravaggio paintings, and urban showstoppers such as Piazza Navona (plus the Pantheon). The fifth itinerary goes deep into Rome's postcard-country of the Spanish Steps and the Trevi Fountain. The next itinerary brings you to three of Rome's most historic churches (and Michelangelo's *Moses*). The following itinerary is a journey thick with Baroque treasures, including the Palazzo Colonna—Rome's most splendorous palace—and several of Bernini's best sculptures. The eighth walking itinerary ranges from the palatial 17th-century Galleria Borghese to the Villa Medici, home to the city's most poetic gardens. The ninth walk explores the Ghetto and Trastevere, Rome's own "Greenwich Village." Finally we take you from the atmosphere-rich Catacombs to the Appian Way.

Its natives are fond of reminding visitors that Rome wasn't built in a day. Neither can it be seen in a day, or even two or three. Perhaps visitors should be Nero-esque in their rambles—and fiddle while they roam: People who occasionally stop for a cappuccino get more out of these breaks than those who breathlessly try to make every second count. After all, there is no way to see everything. The Italian author Silvio Negro said it best: *"Roma, non basta una vita"* (Rome, a lifetime is not enough).

Ancient Rome: Glories of the Caesars

This walk takes you through the very core of Roman antiquity, through what was once the epicenter of the known world, the Roman Forum, and gives you a look at how Michelangelo transformed the Capitoline Hill—the seat of ancient Rome's government—into a Renaissance showcase. The rubblescape of marble fragments scattered over the area of the Forum makes all but students of archeology ask: Is this the grandeur that was Rome? Just consider that much of the history fed to students the world over happened right here. This square—once an enormous banquet hall where the entire population of a city could be simultaneously entertained (as our times have observed thanks to such Hollywood epics as *Quo Vadis, Ben-Hur,* and *Cleopatra*)—was the birthplace for much of Western civilization. Roman law and powerful armies were created here, banishing the barbarian world for a millennium. Here, all Rome shouted as one, "Caesar has been murdered," and crowded to hear Mark Antony's eulogy for the fallen leader. Legend has it that St. Paul traversed the Forum en route to his audience with Nero. After a more than 27-century-long parade of pageantry, it is not surprising that Shelley and Gibbon had their dreams of *Sic transit gloria mundi* on these same grounds.

A Good Walk
Numbers in the text correspond to numbers in the margin and on the Rome and Old Rome: The Historic Center maps.

Rome, as everyone knows, was built on seven hills. Begin your walk at the **Capitoline Hill** ①—the site of Michelangelo's spectacular piazza and Rome's City Hall, **Palazzo Senatorio,** which was built over the Tabularium, the ancient hall of records. Flanking the palazzo are both halves of Rome's most noteworthy museum complex, the **Musei Capitolini** ②, made up of the **Museo Capitolino** and the **Palazzo dei Conservatori,** which contain works of art gathered by Pope Sixtus V, one of the earliest papal patrons of the arts. Off to the side of the Capitoline, at the head of its formidable flight of steep steps, stands the ancient redbrick church of **Santa Maria d'Aracoeli** ③. Below the gardens to the left of the Palazzo Senatorio are **Caesar's Forum** and the forum named after the Emperor Trajan, separated by Via dei Fori Imperiali; the latter contains the ruins of **Trajan's Column** ④. Descend Via San Pietro in Carcere, actually a flight of stairs, to the gloomy **Mamertine Prison** ⑤ and the **Roman Forum** ⑥, continuing along Via dei Fori Imperiali where, on the right, you will come across the **Palatine Hill** ⑦, site of Rome's earliest settlement. Leaving the Palatine by way of the San Gregorio exit, you'll come upon the imposing **Arch of Constantine** ⑧ and, beyond it, the **Colosseum** ⑨, one of antiquity's most famous monuments. Don't forget to check out the ruins of Nero's **Domus Aurea** ⑩, his sumptuous palace, behind the Colosseum.

TIMING

It takes about 30 minutes to walk the route, plus two hours to visit the Capitoline Museums, two to three hours to explore the Roman Forum and Palatine, and 20 minutes to an hour to see the Colosseum.

Sights to See

Numbers in the margin correspond to points of interest on the Rome map.

⑧ Arch of Constantine. This imposing arch was erected in AD 315 to celebrate Constantine's victory over Maxentius. Not only is it the best preserved of Rome's triumphal arches, it is also the largest (69 feet high, 85 feet wide, and 23 feet deep) and one of the last great monuments of ancient Rome. It once stood at the head of the Via Sacra, but now stands in glorious isolation alongside the Colosseum (☞ *below*).

OFF THE BEATEN PATH

PROTESTANT CEMETERY – About 20 minutes' walk south from the Arch of Constantine along Viale Aventino, behind the Piramide, a stone pyramid built in 12 BC at the order of the

Exploring Rome

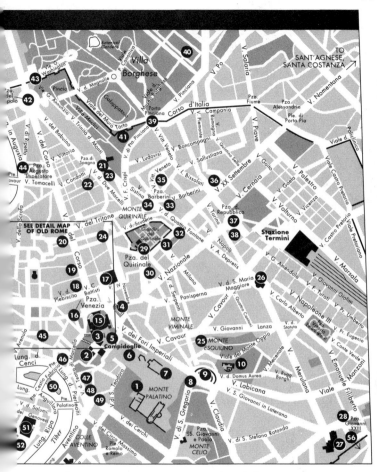

St. Peter's Basilica, **13**

Sant'Ignazio, **19**

Santa Cecilia in Trastevere, **51**

Santa Maria d'Aracoeli, **3**

Santa Maria del Popolo, **43**

Santa Maria della Concezione, **35**

Santa Maria della Vittoria, **36**

Santa Maria Maggiore, **26**

San Carlo alle Quattro Fontane, **32**

San Francesco a Ripa, **52**

San Giovanni in Laterano, **27**

San Pietro in Montorio, **55**

San Pietro in Vincoli, **25**

Sant'Andrea, **31**

Scala Santa, **28**

Spanish Steps, **21**

Teatro di Marcello, **46**

Temple of Fortuna Virlis, **47**

Temple of Vesta, **48**

Tiberina Island, **50**

Trajan's Column, **4**

Trevi Fountain, **24**

Tritone Fountain, **34**

Vatican Museums, **14**

Via Appia Antica, **56**

Villa Farnesina, **54**

Vittorio Emanuele Monument, **15**

Roman *praetor* (senior magistrate) who was buried there, is a cemetery reminiscent of a country churchyard. Among the headstones you'll find Keats's tomb and the place where Shelley's heart was buried. ✉ *Via Caio Cestio 6,* ☎ *06/ 574-1141 (ring bell for custodian).* 🎟 *Offering of 500 lire–1,000 lire.* 🕐 *Daily 8–11:30 and 3:20–5:30.*

Caesar's Forum. This is the oldest of the Imperial Fora, those built by the emperors as opposed to those built during the earlier, Republican period (6th–1st centuries BC) as part of the original Roman Forum.

★ ❶ **Capitoline Hill.** Though most of the buildings on Michelangelo's piazza date from the Renaissance, the hill was once the epicenter of the Roman Empire, the place where the city's first and holiest temples stood, including its most sacred, the Temple of Jupiter. The city's archives were kept in the Tabularium (hall of records), the tall, gray-stone structure that forms the foundation of today's city hall, **Palazzo Senatorio.** By the Middle Ages, the Campidoglio, as the hill was already called then, had fallen into ruin. In 1537, Pope Paul III decided to restore its grandeur for the triumphal entry into the city of Charles V, the Holy Roman Emperor, and called upon Michelangelo to create the staircase ramp; the buildings on three sides of the Campidoglio Square; the slightly convex pavement and its decoration; and the pedestal for the bronze equestrian statue of Marcus Aurelius. A work from the 2nd century AD, the statue stood here from the 16th century until 1981. The statue—the most celebrated equestrian bronze to survive from classical antiquity—was mistakenly believed to represent the Christian emperor Constantine rather than the pagan Marcus Aurelius, hence its survival through the centuries. A legend foretells that some day the statue's original gold patina will return, heralding the end of the world. To forestall destiny, the city fathers had it restored and placed in Palazzo dei Conservatori (☞ *below*), saving not only what was left of the gold, but also the statue's bronze, once seriously menaced by air pollution. A copy of the statue may be set up outdoors by 1997, installed on the original pedestal. As Michelangelo's preeminent urban set piece, the piazza sums up all the majesty of High-Renaissance Rome.

★ ⑨ **Colosseum.** Massive and majestic, ancient Rome's most famous monument was begun by the Flavian emperor Vespasian in AD 72, and inaugurated eight years later with a program of games and shows lasting 100 days. More than 50,000 spectators could sit within the arena's 573-yard circumference, which was faced with marble, accented with hundreds of statues, and had the velarium—an ingenious system of sail-like awnings rigged on ropes manned by sailors culled from imperial warships—to protect the audience from the sun and rain. Before the imperial box, gladiators would salute the emperor and cry, *"Ave, imperator, morituri te salutant"* (Hail, emperor, men soon to die salute thee); it is said that when one day they heard the emperor Claudius respond, "or maybe not," they became so offended that they called a strike. Although originally known as the Flavian Amphitheater, it was called the Colosseum by later Romans, as reported by the Venerable Bede in 730, after a truly colossal gilded bronze statue of Nero in the vicinity that stood until the end of the 6th century. The arena later served as a quarry from which materials were filched to build Renaissance-era churches and palaces. Finally, it was declared sacred by the Vatican in memory of the many Christians believed martyred there (scholars now maintain that no Christians met their death in the Colosseum, but rather in Rome's imperial circuses). During the 19th century, romantic poets lauded the glories of the amphitheater when viewed by moonlight. Now its arches glow at night with mellow golden spotlights, less romantic, perhaps, but still unforgettable. Portions of the arena will be closed during ongoing restoration. ✉ *Piazza del Colosseo,* ☎ *06/700–4261.* ▣ *General admission free, upper levels 8,000 lire.* ☺ *Apr.–Sept., Mon., Tues., Thurs.–Sat. 9–7, Wed. and Sun. 9–1; Oct.–Mar., Mon., Tues., Thurs.–Sat 9–3, Wed. and Sun. 9–1.*

NEED A BREAK?	About half a block from the Colosseum is **Pasqualino** (✉ Via Santi Quattro 66), a reasonably priced neighborhood trattoria with a few sidewalk tables providing a view of the arena's marble arches. The restaurant is closed Monday. For delicious ice cream try **Ristoro della Salute** (✉ Piazza del Colosseo 2a), one of Rome's best *gelaterie* (ice-cream parlors).

⑩ Domus Aurea. On the Colle Oppio (Oppian Hill), a ridge of the Esquiline Hill, is what's left of Nero's sumptuous palace—later buried under Trajan's Baths—which was built after the great fire of AD 64 destroyed much of the city. (Incidentally, historians now believe Nero to be blameless in this event.) Also known as the Golden House, it was a structure so huge it evoked the complaint, "All Rome has become a villa."

❺ Mamertine Prison. This series of gloomy, subterranean cells is where Rome's vanquished enemies were finished off. Some historians believe that St. Peter was held prisoner here, and legend has it that he miraculously brought forth a spring of water with which to baptize his jailers. 📧 *Donation requested.* ☉ *Daily 9–12:30 and 2–7:30.*

❷ Musei Capitolini. The collections in the twin Museo Capitolino and Palazzo dei Conservatori were assembled in the 15th century by Pope Sixtus V, one of the earliest of the great papal patrons of the arts. Although parts of the collection may excite only archaeologists and art historians, others contain some of the most famous—and not to be missed—pieces of classical sculpture, such as the poignant *Dying Gaul*, the regal *Capitoline Venus* (recently identified as another Mediterranean beauty, Cleopatra herself), and the delicate *Marble Faun* that inspired 19th-century novelist Nathaniel Hawthorne's novel of the same name. Remember that many of the works here and in Rome's other museums were copied from Greek originals. For hundreds of years, craftsmen of ancient Rome prospered by producing copies of Greek statues, using a process called "pointing," by which exact replicas could be created to order.

Portraiture, however, was one area in which the Romans outstripped the Greeks. The hundreds of Roman portrait busts in the Sala degli Imperatori and Sala dei Filosofi of the **Museo Capitolino** constitute an ancient *Who's Who*. Within these serried ranks are 48 of the Roman emperors, ranging from Augustus (died AD 14) to Theodosius (died 395). Many of them were eminently forgettable, but some were men of genius; a few added nothing to the Roman way of life except new ways of dying. On one console, you'll see the handsomely austere Augustus, who "found Rome a city of brick and left it one of marble." On another rests

Claudius "the stutterer," an indefatigable builder brought vividly to life in Robert Graves's *I, Claudius*. In this company is also Nero, most notorious of the emperors—though by no means the worst—who built for himself the fabled Domus Aurea (☞ *above*). And, of course, the baddies: cruel Caligula and Caracalla, and the dissolute, eerily modern boy-emperor, Heliogabalus.

Unlike the Greeks, whose portraits are idealized and usually beautiful, the Romans belonged to the "warts and all" school of representation. Many of the busts that have come down to us, seen clearly in that of Commodus, the emperor-gladiator (found in a gallery on the upper level of the museum), are nearly savage in the relentlessness of their portrayals. As you leave the museum, be sure to stop in the courtyard at the gigantic, reclining figure of Oceanus, found in the Roman Forum and later dubbed Marforio, one of Rome's famous "talking statues" to which citizens from the 1500s up to the 20th century affixed anonymous notes of political protest and satirical verses.

The **Palazzo dei Conservatori** is a trove of ancient and Baroque treasures. Lining the courtyard are the colossal fragments of a head, leg, foot, and hand, all that remains of the famous statue of the emperor Constantine the Great, who believed that Rome's future in the 3rd century AD lay with Christianity; these immense effigies were much in vogue in the later days of the Roman empire. The resplendent Salone dei Orazi e Curiazi on the first floor is a ceremonial hall with a magnificent gilt ceiling, carved wooden doors, and 16th-century frescoes. At either end of the hall reign statues of the Baroque Age's most charismatic popes, Bernini's marble effigy of Urban VIII and his rival Algardi's bronze statue of Innocent X. World-renowned symbol of Rome, the *Capitoline Wolf*, a 6th-century-BC Etruscan bronze, has a place of honor in the museum; the suckling twins were added during the Renaissance to adapt the statue to the legend of Romulus and Remus. ⊠ *Museo Capitolino and Palazzo dei Conservatori, Piazza del Campidoglio,* ☎ *06/671–002475.* ▣ *10,000 lire, free last Sun. of month.* ☉ *May–Sept., Tues. 9–1:30 and 5–8, Wed.–Fri. 9–1:30, Sat. 9–1:30 and 8–11, Sun. 9–1; Oct.–Apr., Tues. and Sat. 9–1:30 and 5–8, Wed.–Fri. 9–1:30, Sun. 9–1.*

❼ Palatine Hill. The Clivus Palatinus (as it was known in Latin), whose worn paving stones were once trod by emperors and their slaves, is where historians point to Rome's earliest settlement. About a century ago, Rome's greatest archaeologist, Rodolfo Lanciani, excavated a site on the Palatine Hill—and found evidence testifying to Romulus's historical presence, thereby contradicting early critics who deemed Romulus to be a myth. The story goes that the twins Romulus and Remus were abandoned as infants but were suckled by a she wolf on the banks of the Tiber and adopted by a shepherd. Encouraged by the gods to build a city, the twins chose a site in 735 BC, fortifying it with a wall that Lanciani identified by digging on the Palatine. During the building of the city, the brothers quarreled, and in a fit of anger Romulus killed Remus.

Despite its location overlooking the Forum with its extreme traffic congestion and attendant noise, the Palatine was the most coveted address for ancient Rome's rich and famous. More than a few of the 12 Caesars called the Palatine home—including Caligula, who met his premature end in the still-standing and unnerving—even today—tunnel, the Cryptoporticus. The palace of Tiberius was the first to be built here; others followed, most notably the gigantic extravaganza constructed for emperor Domitian.

In the **Circus Maximus,** the giant arena laid out between the Palatine and Aventine hills, more than 300,000 spectators watched chariot races while the emperor surveyed the scene from his palace on the Palatine Hill.

❻ Roman Forum. In what was once a marshy valley between the Capitoline and Palatine hills, this was the civic heart of Republican Rome, the austere enclave that preceded the hedonistic society that grew up under the emperors in the 1st to the 4th century AD. Today it seems no more than a baffling series of ruins, marble fragments, isolated columns, a few worn arches, and occasional paving stones. Yet it once was filled with stately and extravagant buildings—temples, palaces, shops—and crowded with people from all corners of the world. What you see today are the ruins not of one period, but of almost 900 years, from about 500 BC to AD 400. Making sense of these scarred and pitted stones is not easy; you may want just to wander along, letting your imagination dwell on Cicero, Julius Caesar, and Mark Antony, who delivered the funeral address in Caesar's honor from the rostrum just left of the **Arch of Septimius Severus.**

In addition to this arch—one of the grandest of all antiquity, it was built in AD 203 to celebrate the emperor Severus's victory over the Parthians, and was topped by a bronze equestrian statuary group with no fewer than six horses—most visitors explore the large brick senate hall, the **Curia,** which survives as it was in the era of Diocletian in the late 3rd century AD; the three Corinthian columns (a favorite of 19th-century poets)—all that remains of the **Temple of Vespasian;** the circular **Temple of Vesta,** where the highly privileged vestal virgins kept the sacred flame alive; and the **Arch of Titus,** which stands in a slightly elevated position on a spur of the Palatine Hill. The view of the Colosseum from the arch is superb, and reminds us that it was the emperor Titus who helped finish the vast amphitheater, begun earlier by his father, Vespasian. Now cleaned and restored, the arch was erected in AD 81 to celebrate the sack of Jerusalem 10 years earlier, after the great Jewish revolt. A famous relief shows the captured contents of Herod's Temple—including its huge seven-branched menorah—being carried in triumph down Rome's Via Sacra. ⊠ *Entrances on Via dei Fori Imperiali, Piazza Santa Maria Nova, and Via di San Gregorio,* ☎ *06/699–0110.* ⌂ *12,000 lire.* ☉ *Apr.–Sept., Mon.–Sat. 9–6, Sun. 9–1; Oct.–Mar., Mon.–Sat. 9–3, Sun. 9–1.*

❸ Santa Maria d'Aracoeli. This stark, redbrick church is one of the first Christian churches in Rome. Legend recounts that it was on this spot that the Sybil predicted to Augustus the coming of a Redeemer. The emperor responded by erecting the Ara Coeli—the Altar of Heaven. The Aracoeli is best known for Pinturicchio's 15th-century frescoes in the first chapel on the right and for the **Santa Bambino,** a much-revered wooden figure of the Christ Child (today a copy of the 15th-century original). During the Christmas season, children recite poems from a miniature pulpit here. ⊠ *Piazza d'Aracoeli.* ☉ *Oct. 1–May 31, daily 7–12 and 4–6; June 1–Sept., 30 daily 7–12 and 4–6:30.*

❹ **Trajan's Column,** in the base of which Emperor Trajan's ashes were buried, stands in what was once **Trajan's Forum,** with its huge semicircular market building, adjacent to the ruins of the **Forum of Augustus.**

The Vatican: Rome of the Popes

The Vatican is a place where some people go to find a work of art—Michelangelo's frescoes, rare archaeological marbles, or Bernini's statues. Others go to find their souls. In between these two extremes lies an awe-inspiring landscape that offers a famous sight for every taste and inclination. Rooms decorated by Raphael, antique sculptures like the *Apollo Belvedere* and the *Laocoön,* walls daubed by Fra Angelico, famous paintings by Giotto and Leonardo, and chief among revered *non plus ultras,* the ceiling of the Sistine Chapel: For the lover of beauty, few places are as historically important as this epitome of faith and grandeur. What gave all this impetus was a new force that emerged as the emperors of ancient Rome presided over their declining empire: Christianity came to Rome, and the seat of the popes was established over the tomb of St. Peter, thereby making the Vatican the spiritual core of the Roman Catholic Church. Today, there are two principal reasons for seeing the Vatican. One is to visit St. Peter's, the largest church in the world and the most overwhelming architectural achievement of the Renaissance; the other is to visit the Vatican Museums, which contain collections of staggering richness and diversity.

A Good Walk

Start your walk at the **Castel Sant'Angelo** ⑪, the fortress that once guarded the Vatican, and take in the angel-studded beauty of the **Ponte Sant'Angelo** before turning right onto Via della Conciliazione (or taking a more picturesque route along Borgo Pio) to the Vatican. Once inside **Piazza San Pietro** ⑫ you are inside Vatican territory, and a feast of artistic delights awaits you: **St. Peter's Basilica** ⑬, the largest church in Christendom. To the right as you enter you'll find Michelangelo's stunning *Pietà;* of the many treasures to be seen, be sure not to miss the Historical Museum in the Sacristy, the excavations below the church, the

Vatican gardens, and the Vatican Grottoes, the last repose of the popes. Finally, the Vatican is where millions of Catholics (and, indeed, many non-Catholics) come in hope of a **papal audience**; the chance to see the pope in person is for many the highlight of a trip to Rome.

TIMING

Allow two hours for a visit to Castel Sant'Angelo. The walk from Castel Sant'Angelo to St. Peter's takes about 30 minutes. You'll need an hour to see St. Peter's, plus 30 minutes for the Historical Museum, 15 minutes for the Vatican Grottoes, 30 minutes to visit the roof, and an hour to climb to the lantern. To avoid the crowds, get to St. Peter's early in the morning, at lunchtime, or in the late afternoon.

Sights to See

11 Castel Sant'Angelo. For hundreds of years this fortress guarded the Vatican, to which it is linked by the Passetto, an arcaded passageway. Anyone harboring doubts as to the almost unimaginable wealth and power of ancient Rome's emperors will have them dashed here: Though it may look like a stronghold, Castel Sant'Angelo was in fact built as a tomb for the emperor Hadrian in AD 135. By the 6th century, it had been transformed into a fortress, and it remained a refuge for the popes for almost 1,000 years. It has dungeons, battlements, cannons and cannonballs, and a collection of antique weaponry and armor.

One of Rome's most beautiful bridges, **Ponte Sant'Angelo** spans the Tiber in front of the fortress and is studded with graceful angels designed by Giovanni Lorenzo Bernini (1598–1680).

According to legend, the Castel Sant'Angelo got its name during the plague of 590, when Pope Gregory the Great, passing by in a religious procession, had a vision of an angel sheathing its sword atop the stone ramparts. The lower levels formed the base of Hadrian's mausoleum; ancient ramps and narrow staircases climb through the castle's core to courtyards and frescoed halls and rooms holding a collection of antique arms and armor. Off the loggia is a café. The upper terrace, below the massive bronze angel commemorating Gregory's vision, evokes memories of Tosca, Puccini's poignant heroine in the opera of the same name, who threw herself off these ramparts with the cry, *"Scarpia, avanti a Dio!"* ("Scarpia, we meet before God!"). ⊠ *Lungotevere Castello 50,* ☎ *06/687–5036.* 🖾 *8,000 lire.* ⊙ *Mon.–Sat. 9–2, Sun. 9–noon; closed 2nd and 4th Tues. of month.*

⑫   **Piazza San Pietro (St. Peter's Square).** As you enter the square you are entering Vatican territory. This square (actually an oval) is one of Bernini's most spectacular masterpieces. Completed in 1667, after 11 years' work—a relatively short time in those days, considering the vastness of the task—the square can hold 400,000 people. It is surrounded by a curving pair of quadruple colonnades, which are topped by a balustrade and statues of 140 saints. Look for the two stone disks set into the pavement on each side of the obelisk. If you stand on one disk, a trick of perspective makes the colonnades seem to consist of a single row of columns. Bernini had an even grander visual effect in mind when he designed the square. By opening up this immense, airy, and luminous space in a neighborhood of narrow, shadowy streets, he created a contrast that would surprise and impress anyone who emerged from the darkness into the light, in a characteristically Baroque metaphor. But in the 1930's, Mussolini ruined it all. To celebrate the "conciliation" between the Vatican and the Italian government under the Lateran Pact of 1929, he conceived of Via della Conciliazione, the broad, rather soulless avenue that now forms the main approach to St. Peter's and gives the eye time to adjust to the enormous dimensions of the square and church, ruining Bernini's grand Baroque effect.

★ ⑬   **St. Peter's Basilica.** Most viewers find this, the largest church of Christendom, to be one of Rome's most impressive sights. The physical statistics are imposing: It covers about 18,100 square yards, runs 212 yards in length, and carries a dome that rises 435 feet and measures 138 feet across its base. Its history is equally impressive: No fewer than five of Italy's greatest artists—Bramante, Raphael, Peruzzi, Antonio Sangallo the Younger, and Michelangelo—died while striving to erect this new St. Peter's. The history of the original St. Peter's goes back to the year AD 319, when the emperor Constantine built a basilica over the site of the tomb of St. Peter. This early church stood for more than 1,000 years, undergoing a number of restorations, until it was on the verge of collapse. Reconstruction began in 1452, but was abandoned due to a lack of funds. In 1506 Pope Julius II instructed the architect Donato Bramante (1444–1514) to raze the existing structure and build a new and greater basilica, but it wasn't until 1626 that the new church was completed and dedicated. In 1546 Pope Paul III persuaded the aging Michelangelo to take on the job of completing the building. Returning to Bramante's ground plan, Michelangelo designed the dome to cover the crossing, but his plans, too, were modified after his death. The cupola, one of the most beautiful in the world, was completed by Della Porta and Fontana. Under the portico, Filarete's 15th-century bronze doors, salvaged from the old basilica, are in the central portal. Ushers at the entrance will not allow persons wearing shorts, miniskirts, sleeveless T-shirts, or other revealing clothing (it's advisable for women to carry a scarf to cover bare shoulders and upper arms) into St. Peter's church. Off the entry portico, Bernini's famous *Scala Regia,* the ceremonial entryway to the Vatican Palace—the residence of the pope—and one of the most magnificent staircases in the world, is graced with Bernini's dramatic statue of Constantine the Great.

The cherubs over the holy water fonts will give you an idea of just how huge St. Peter's is: the sole of the cherub's foot is as long as the distance from your fingers to your elbow. It is because the proportions of this giant building are in such perfect harmony that its vastness may escape you at first. But in its megascale—inspired by the spatial volumes of ancient Roman ruins—it reflects Roman *grandiosità* in all its majesty.

Over an altar in a side chapel is Michelangelo's **Pietà**. It is difficult to determine whether this moving work, sculpted when he was only 22, owes more to the man's art than to his faith. As we contemplate this masterpiece we are able to understand a little better that art and faith sometimes partake of the same impulse.

Four massive piers support the dome at the crossing, where the mighty Bernini **baldacchino** (canopy) rises high above the papal altar. "What the barbarians didn't do, the Barberini did," 17th-century wags quipped when Barberini Pope

Urban VIII had the bronze stripped from the Pantheon's portico and melted down to make the baldacchino (using what was left over for cannonballs). The pope celebrates mass here, over the grottoes holding the tombs of many of his predecessors. Also here, deep in the excavations under the foundations of the original basilica, is what is believed to be the tomb of St. Peter. The bronze throne above the main altar in the apse, the Cathedra Petri, is Bernini's work (1656) and it covers a wooden and ivory chair that St. Peter himself is said to have used. However, scholars tell us that this throne probably dates only to the Middle Ages. We come to these contradictions often. Faith, in the end, outweighs authenticity when it is a question of sacred objects. See how the adoration of a million lips has completely worn down the bronze on the right foot of the statue of St. Peter near the crossing.

The scale of the aisles and decoration and the vast sweep of the dome over the ceremonial entrance to the crypt, which is surrounded by votive lamps, bring home the point that St. Peter's is much more than a church; it was intended to function as the glorious setting for all the pomp and panoply of ecclesiastical ceremony. Indeed, only when it serves as the brightly lit background for a great gathering do its vast dimensions find their full expression.

A small but rich collection of Vatican treasures is housed in the **Historical Museum** in the Sacristy, among them precious antique chalices and the massive 15th-century sculptured bronze tomb of Pope Sixtus V by Antonio Pollaiuolo (1429–98). ▣ *3,000 lire.* ۩ *Apr.–Sept., daily 9–6:30; Oct.–Mar., daily 9–5:30.*

The entrance to the **Vatican Grottoes,** which hold the tombs of many popes, is at the crossing. The only exit from the grottoes leads outside St. Peter's, to the courtyard that holds the entrance to the roof and dome. ▣ *Free.* ۩ *Apr.–Sept., daily 7–6; Oct.–Mar., daily 7–5.*

The **roof** of the church, reached by elevator or stairs, is an interesting landscape of domes and towers. A short interior staircase leads to the base of the dome for a dove's-eye view of the interior of the church. Only if you are stout of heart and sound of lung should you attempt the very taxing and claustrophobic climb up the narrow stairs—there's no turning back!—to the balcony of the lantern, where the view embraces the Vatican gardens as well as all of Rome. ▨ *Elevator 6,000 lire, stairs 5,000 lire.* ⊗ *Apr.–Sept., daily 8–6; Oct.–Mar., daily 8–5.*

OFF THE BEATEN PATH	**EXCAVATIONS** - Visit these under St. Peter's for a fascinating glimpse of the underpinnings of the great basilica, which was built over the cemetery where archaeologists say they have found St. Peter's tomb. Apply a few days in advance (or try in the morning for the same day) to Ufficio Scavi (Excavations Office), on the right beyond the Arco delle Campane entrance to Vatican, which is left of the basilica. Tell the Swiss guard you want the Ufficio Scavi, and he will let you by. ☎ *06/6988-5318.* ▨ *Guide 10,000 lire, audiotape tour 6,000 lire.* ⊗ *Ufficio Scavi Mon.–Sat. 9–5.*
NEED A BREAK?	Borgo Pio, a street a block or two from St. Peter's Square, has several trattorias offering economical tourist menus. For about 20,000 lire you can have a simple meal at **Il Pozzetto** (✉ Borgo Pio 167). The restaurant is closed Monday. The tiny **Dolceborgo** pastry shop (✉ Borgo Pio 162) is the place to go for cookies and creamy concoctions.

Papal Audience. For many, this is a highlight of a trip to Rome. John Paul II, 264th Pope of the Roman Catholic Church, holds mass audiences on Wednesday mornings at 11, in a large modern audience hall or in St. Peter's Square in summer, if it's not too hot. You must apply for tickets in advance; there are several sources (☞ *below*), but if you are pressed for time it may be easier to arrange for them through a travel agency. Of course, you can avoid the formalities by seeing the pope when he makes his weekly appearance at the window of the Vatican Palace, every Sunday at noon when he is in Rome, to address the crowd and give a blessing. On summer Sundays he may give the blessing at his summer residence at Castel Gandolfo. For audience tickets apply in writing well in advance to Prefettura della Casa Pontificia (✉ 00120 Vatican City), indicating the date you prefer, the language you speak, and the hotel where you will be staying. Or go to the prefecture (☎ 06/

6982), through the bronze door in the right-hand colonnade; the office is open Monday and Tuesday 9–1 for the Wednesday audience, although last-minute tickets may be available. You can also pick up free tickets at North American College (⊠ Via dell'Umiltà 30, ☎ 06/678–9184) and through Santa Susanna American Church (⊠ Piazza San Bernardo, ☎ 06/482–7510). For a fee, travel agencies make arrangements that include transportation (☞ Guided Tours *in* Rome A to Z, *below*).

The **Vatican gardens** tour offers a two-hour jaunt through the pope's backyard, half by bus and half on foot, with a guide. Tickets are available at the Vatican Information Office (⊠ Piazza San Pietro, ☎ 06/ 6988–4466). Make reservations two or three days in advance. ☜ 16,000 lire. ☺ Sat. at 10.

The Vatican Museums: More than Just the Sistine Ceiling

The Vatican Palace has been the residence of Popes since 1377. Actually, it represents a collection of buildings that cover more than 13 acres, containing an estimated (no one has bothered to count them) 1,400 rooms, chapels, and galleries. Other than the Pope and his papal court, the occupants are some of the most famous art masterpieces in the world. The main entrance to the museums, on Viale Vaticano, is a long walk from Piazza San Pietro, but there is bus service between the St. Peter's Square information office and a secondary museum entrance. The bus goes through the Vatican gardens and costs 2,000 lire, and although it deposits you at a side entrance, it saves a lot of walking and allows a glimpse of some of Vatican City that would be off-limits otherwise. Some city buses stop near the museums' main entrance on Viale Vaticano: Bus 49 from Piazza Cavour stops right in front; Bus 80 and Tram 19 stop at Piazza Risorgimento, halfway between St. Peter's and the museums. The Ottaviano stop on Metro A also is in the vicinity.

A Good Walk

For many, the highlight of any visit to the **Vatican Museums** ⑭ is the **Sistine Chapel**. Not to be overlooked, however, are the recently rearranged **Egyptian Museum** and the

Chiaramonti and Pio Clementino Museums, which are given over to classical sculptures (among them some of the best-known statues in the world—the *Laocoön,* the *Belvedere Torso,* and the *Apollo Belvedere*—works that, with their vibrant humanism, had a tremendous impact on Renaissance art), and the Etruscan Museum and three other sections of special interest. Finally, you should make sure to visit the Candelabra Gallery and the Tapestry Gallery, which is hung with magnificent tapestries executed from Raphael's designs.

TIMING

The shortest itinerary takes approximately 90 minutes; others take three hours and 3½ hours, and the longest takes 4½ hours. To avoid the crowds, get there before opening time, or go at lunchtime or in the last few hours before closing.

Sights to See

🄬 **Vatican Museums.** The immense collections housed here are so rich that unless you are an art history fan, you will probably want to just skim the surface, concentrating on pieces that strike your fancy. The Sistine Chapel is a must, of course, and that's why you may have to wait on line to see it; after all, every tourist in Rome has the same idea. Pick up a leaflet at the main entrance to the museums in order to see the overall layout. Special posters at the entrance and throughout the museums plot a choice of four color-coded itineraries. The Sistine Chapel is at the far end of the complex, and the leaflet charts two abbreviated itineraries through other collections to reach it. You can rent a taped commentary in English explaining the Sistine Chapel and the Raphael Rooms. Below, we give some of the highlights, whether or not you follow the itineraries suggested by the curators.

The Gallery of Maps is intriguing; the Apartment of Pius V, a little less so. The Stanze di Raffaello (the Raphael Rooms), are second only to the Sistine Chapel in artistic interest. In 1508, Pope Julius II employed Raphael Sanzio, on the recommendation of Bramante, to decorate the rooms with biblical scenes. The result was a Renaissance masterpiece. Of the four rooms, the second and third were decorated mainly by Raphael; here are his exceptional *Transfiguration, Coronation,* and *Foligno Madonna.* The others were decorated by Giulio Romano and other assistants of Raphael; the first room is known as the Incendio Room, with frescoes painted by Romano. It's hard to overstate the importance of the **Segnatura Room (the Room of the Signature);** here papal bulls were signed. When people talk about the High Renaissance—thought by many to be the pinnacle of Western art—these frescoes often come to mind. The theme of the room—which may broadly be said to be "enlightenment"—reflects the fact that this was Julius's private library. Theology triumphs in the fresco known as the *Disputa,* or *Debate on the Holy Sacrament.* The *School of Athens* glorifies some of philosophy's greatest exponents, including Plato and Socrates at the fresco's center. The pensive figure on the stairs is sometimes thought to be modeled on Michelangelo, who was painting the Sistine Ceiling at the same time Raphael was working here. All the revolutionary characteristics of High Renaissance paintings are here: naturalism (Raphael's figures lack the awkwardness that pictures painted only a few years earlier still contained); humanism (the idea that man is the most noble and admirable of God's creatures); and a profound interest in the ancient world, the result of the 15th-century rediscovery of archaeology and classical antiquity. There's a tendency to go into something of a stupor when confronted with "great art" of this kind. The fact remains that the frescoes in this room virtually dared its occupants to aspire to the highest ideas of law and learning—an amazing feat for an artist not yet 30.

The tiny **Chapel of Nicholas V** is aglow with frescoes by Fra Angelico (1387–1455), the Florentine monk whose sensitive paintings were guiding lights for the Renaissance. The **Borgia Apartments** are worth seeing for their elaborately painted ceilings, designed and partially executed by Pinturicchio (1454–1513), but the rooms have been given over to the Vatican's large, but not particularly interesting, collection of modern religious art.

In 1508, while Raphael was put to work on his series of rooms, the redoubtable Pope Julius II commissioned Michelangelo to fresco the more than 10,000 square feet

★ of the **Sistine Chapel** ceiling singlehandedly. The task took four years of mental and physical anguish. It's said that for years afterward Michelangelo couldn't read anything without holding it up over his head. The result, however, was the masterpiece that you can now see, its colors cool and brilliant after recent restoration. Bring a pair of binoculars to get a better look at this incredible work (unfortunately, you're not allowed to lie down on the floor to study the frescoes above, the viewing position of choice in decades past; by the time you leave the chapel, your neck may feel like Michelangelo's, so you may also want to study it—to take a cue from 19th-century visitors—with the aid of a pocket mirror). The ceiling is literally a painted Bible: Michelangelo's subject was the story of humanity before the coming of Christ, seen through Augustinian tenets of faith popular in early 16th-century theological circles. While some of the frescoed panels are veritable stews of figures, others—especially the depiction of God's outstretched hand giving Adam the spark of life in the *Creation of Adam*—are majestically simple, revealing how much art Michelangelo brought to the field of painting from the discipline of sculpture. In 1541, some 30 years after completing the ceiling, Michelangelo was commissioned to paint the *Last Judgment* on the wall over the altar. If the artist's ceiling may be taken as an expression of the optimism of the High Renaissance, the *Last Judgment,* by contrast, is a veritable guided tour through Hell. Not surprisingly, since in the intervening years Rome had been sacked and pillaged by the French (who, in fact, had used the Sistine Chapel to stable their horses).

In the interim, the grim Counter Reformation movement had been adopted by the Church, and the papal court was now so offended by the nakedness of Michelangelo's *Last Judgment* figures that they hired artist Daniele da Volterra—forever after known as *il braghettone* (the breeches-maker)—to paint loincloths over the offending parts. The aged and embittered artist painted his own face on the wrinkled human skin in the hand of St. Bartholomew, below and to the right of the figure of Christ, which he clearly modeled on the *Apollo Belvedere* (now on exhibit in the Vatican galleries). Like the ceiling, the *Last Judgment* has been cleaned, surprising viewers with its clarity and color after restorers unveiled their work in April 1994. Was Michelangelo a master of vibrant color? Or is the "new" Sistine a travesty of Michelangelo's intentions? Opinions remain divided, but most art historians believe the restoration is true to Michelangelo's original vision.

The exhibition halls of the **Vatican Library** are bright with frescoes and contain a sampling of the library's rich collections of precious manuscripts. Room X, Room of the Aldobrandini Marriage, holds a beautiful Roman fresco of a nuptial rite. More classical statues are on view in the new wing. At the Quattro Cancelli, a cafeteria offers a well-earned break. The **Pinacoteca** (Picture Gallery) displays mainly religious paintings by such artists as Giotto, Fra Angelico, and Filippo Lippi.

In the **Pagan Antiquities Museum,** modern display techniques enhance another collection of Greek and Roman sculptures. The **Christian Antiquities Museum** has Early Christian and medieval art (its most famous piece is the 3rd-century AD statue, the *Good Shepherd*). The **Ethnological Museum** shows art and artifacts from exotic places throughout the world. The complete itinerary ends with the **Historical Museum,** whose collection of carriages, uniforms, and arms can be opened by a custodian on request.

In all, the Vatican Museums offer a staggering excursion into the realms of art and history. It's foolhardy to try to see all the collections in one day, and it's doubtful that anyone could be interested in everything on display. Simply aim for an overall impression of the collections' artistic and cultural riches. If you want to delve deeper, you can come back another day. ⊠ *Viale Vaticano,* ☎ *06/698–3333.* ▣ *13,000 lire; free last Sun. of month.* ⊘ *Easter wk and July–Sept., weekdays 8:45–5 (last admission at 4), Sat. 8:45–2; Oct.–June (except Easter), Mon.–Sat. 9–2 (last admission at 1); religious holidays (Jan. 1 and 6, Feb. 11, Mar. 19, Easter Sun. and Mon., May 1, Ascension Thurs., Corpus Christi, June 29, Aug. 15 and 16, Nov. 1, Dec. 8, Dec. 25 and 26) and last Sun. of every month 9–2.*

NEED A   Neighborhood trattorias that are far better and far less pop-
BREAK?   ular with tourists than those opposite the Vatican Museum

entrance include **Hostaria Dino e Toni** (⊠ Via Leone IV 60)—where you can dine on typical Roman fare at moderate, even inexpensive, prices—and **La Caravella** (⊠ Via degli Scipioni 32 at Via Vespasiano, off Piazza Risorgimento), which serves Roman specialties and has pizza on the lunch menu. La Caravella is closed Thursday.

Old Rome: Gold and Grandeur

The neighborhood known as Vecchia Roma (Old Rome) is one of Rome's most beautiful districts, thick with narrow streets with curious names, airy Baroque piazzas, and picturesque courtyards. Occupying the horn of land that pushes the Tiber westward toward the Vatican, it has been an integral part of the city since ancient times, and its position between the Vatican and the Lateran palaces, both seats of papal rule, puts it in the mainstream of Rome's development from the Middle Ages onward. It includes such world-famous sights as the Pantheon—ancient Rome's most perfectly preserved building—but it is mainly an excursion into the 16th and 17th centuries, when Baroque art triumphed in Rome. Today, it boasts some of Rome's most coveted residential addresses.

The most important clue to the Romans is their Baroque art—not its artistic technicalities, but its spirit. When you understand that, you will no longer be a stranger in Rome. Flagrantly emotional, heavily expressive, and sensuously visual, the 17th-century artistic movement known as the Baroque was born in Rome, the creation of three geniuses, the sculptor and architect Gianlorenzo Bernini and the painters Annibale Caracci and Caravaggio. Ranging from the austere drama found in Caravaggio's painted altarpieces to the jewel-encrusted, gold-on-gold decoration of 17th-century Roman palace decoration, the Baroque sought to both shock and delight by upsetting the placid, "correct" rules of the Renaissance masters. By appealing to the emotions, it became a powerful weapon in the hands of the Counter Reformation.

A Good Walk

Numbers in the text correspond to numbers in the margin and on the Old Rome: the Historic Center map.

Old Rome: The Historic District

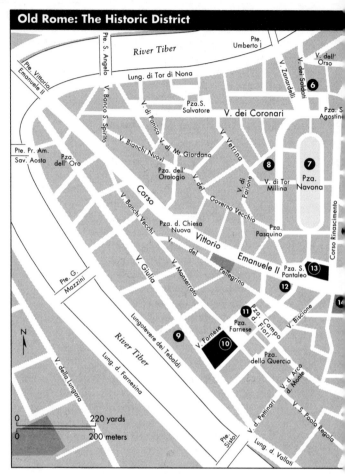

Map labels (as shown):
Pte. Umberto I · River Tiber · Pte. S. Angelo · V. dell' Orso · V. dei Soldati · V. Zanardelli · Pte. Vittorio Emanuele II · Lung. di Tor di Nona · Pza.S. Salvatore · V. dei Coronari · Pza. S Agostine · V. di Panico · V. di Mt. Giordano · V. Vetrina · Pte. Pr. Am. Sav. Aosta · Pza. dell' Oro · V. Bianchi Nuovi · Pza. dell' Orologio · V. di Parione · V. di Tor Millina · Pza. Navona · Corso · V. Banchi Vecchi · V. del Governo Vecchio · Pza. Pasquino · Corso Rinascimento · Pza. d. Chiesa Nuova · Vittorio · Emanuele II · Pza. S. Pantaleo · Pte. G. Mazzini · V. Giulia · V. Monserrato · V. del Pellegrino · Pza. di Campo d. Fiori · V. Biscione · Pza. Farnese · Lungotevere dei Tebaldi · River Tiber · V. Farnese · Pza. della Quercia · V. d. Arco d. Monte · V. della Lungara · Lung. d. Farnesina · V. d. Pettinari · V. S. Paolo Regola · Pte. Sisto · Lung. d. Vallati

N

0 ——— 220 yards
0 ——— 200 meters

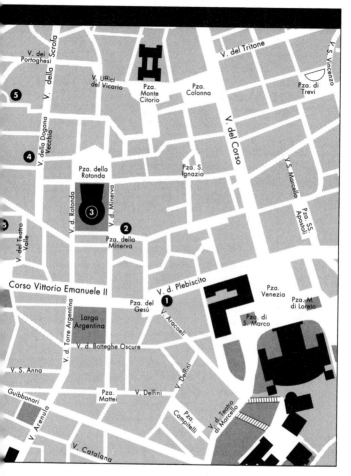

Start on Via del Plebiscito, near Piazza Venezia, at the huge church of **Il Gesù**①, the grandmother of all Baroque churches. Move on to Piazza della Minerva, where in the church of **Santa Maria sopra Minerva** ② you will find the tomb of Fra Angelico. Turn down Via della Minerva to reach the **Pantheon** ③. From Piazza della Rotonda in front of the Pantheon, take Via Giustiniani onto Via della Dogana Vecchia to the church of **San Luigi dei Francesi** ④, a pilgrimage spot for art lovers everywhere. Move on to the church of **Sant'Agostino** ⑤ in the eponymous piazza and the historic **Palazzo Altemps** ⑥, off Piazza Sant'– Apollinaire, before arriving at **Piazza Navona** ⑦, one of Rome's showpiece piazzas, home to Bernini's **Fountain of the Four Rivers** and the church of **Sant'Agnese in Agone,** the quintessence of Baroque architecture. Take Via Tor Millini over to Via della Pace and follow it to Piazza della Pace, where a semicircular portico stands in front of the 15th-century church of **Santa Maria della Pace** ⑧. Explore the byways on that side of Corso Vittorio before crossing over one of Rome's great thoroughfares and making a loop along aristocratic **Via Giulia** to **Palazzo Falconieri** ⑨, and, just ahead, **Palazzo Farnese** ⑩, perhaps the most beautiful Renaissance palace in Rome. On your way back to Corso Vittorio Emanuele, visit the **Campo dei Fiori** ⑪, site of a colorful market, before coming to the **Baracco Museum** ⑫. Across the way, note one of the outstanding architectural monuments of Renaissance Rome, the **Palazzo Massimo alle Colonne** ⑬, and, several blocks along the bustling street, the huge, 17th-century church of **Sant'Andrea della Valle** ⑭. Finally, head down the Corso del Rinascimento to No. 40, the church of **Sant'Ivo alla Sapienza** ⑮, with a golden dome in the shape of a spiral.

TIMING

Allow about three hours for this walk, plus 10 or 15 minutes for each church visited along the way.

Sights to See

⑫ **Baracco Museum.** Housed in a charming little Renaissance town house, this museum features a varied collection of sculptures from ancient Mediterranean civilizations. ⊠ *Via dei Baullari 1,* ☎ *06/688–06848.* ☞ *3,750 lire.* ☉ *Wed., Fri., and Sat. 9–1:30; Tues. and Thurs. 9–1:30 and 5–8, Sun. 9–1.*

⓫ Campo dei Fiori. The best time to visit this square—whose name translates as the Field of Flowers—is on weekday mornings, when the outdoor market fills the square with color and bustle. It was once the scene of public executions (including that of philosopher-monk Giordano Bruno, whose statue broods in the center). ☉ *Mon.–Sat. 7–1:30.*

❶ Il Gesù. Grandmother of all Baroque churches, this huge structure was designed by Vignola in about 1650. The church is the tangible symbol of the power of the Jesuits, who were a major force in the Counter Reformation in Europe. It remained undecorated for about 100 years, but when it finally was decorated, no expense was spared. Its interior drips with gold and lapis lazuli, gold and precious marbles, gold and more gold, all covered by a fantastically painted ceiling by Baciccia that seems to swirl down to merge with the painted stucco figures at its base. ⊠ *Piazza del Gesù.*

❻ Palazzo Altemps. Those interested in ancient sculpture should not miss one of Rome's greatest collections of classical antiquities, housed in this historic building. Opened in 1996, it houses the collections of ancient Roman (and Egyptian) sculpture of the Museo Nazionale Romano. Look for the *Galata,* a poignant work portraying a barbarian warrior who chooses death for himself and his wife rather than humiliation by the enemy, in the famed Ludovisi collection. The palace's stunning early 16th-century courtyard and gorgeously frescoed ceilings make an impressive setting for the sculptures. ⊠ *Via Sant'Apollinare 8,* ☎ *06/683– 3759.* 🎟 *12,000 lire (includes admission to Museo Nazionale delle Terme).*

❾ Palazzo Falconieri. Borromini's masterful work of architecture houses nothing of interest to the visitor, but the building itself makes one of Rome's most elegant attractions. In order to get a good look at this gracefully imposing building, go around the block and view it from along the Tiber embankment. ⊠ *Via Giulia 1.*

❿ Palazzo Farnese. Michelangelo had a hand in building what is now the French Embassy and perhaps the most beautiful Renaissance palace in Rome. Within is the Galleria vault painted by Annibale Carracci between 1597 and 1604— the second-greatest ceiling in Rome; write in advance to the embassy (✉ Ambassador, French Embassy, Piazza Farnese 64, 00186 Rome) for special permission to view it. The Carracci gallery depicts the loves of the gods, a supremely pagan theme that the artist painted in a swirling style that announced the birth of Baroque. It's said that Carracci was so dismayed at the miserly fee he received—the Farnese family was extravagantly rich even by the standards of 15th- and 16th-century Rome's extravagantly rich—that he took to drink and died shortly thereafter. Those who sympathize with the poor man's fate will be further dismayed to learn that the French government pays one lira every 99 years as rent for their sumptuous embassy. ✉ *Piazza Farnese.*

⑬ Palazzo Massimo alle Colonne. A graceful columned portico marks this inconspicuous but seminal architectural monument of Renaissance Rome, built by Baldassare Peruzzi in 1527. Via del Paradiso, around the corner, affords a better view. ✉ *Corso Vittorio Emanuele 141.*

❸ Pantheon. Paradoxically, this is one of Rome's most perfect, best-preserved, and perhaps least-appreciated ancient monuments. Built on the site of an earlier pantheon erected in 27 BC by Augustus's general Agrippa, it was entirely rebuilt by the emperor Hadrian around AD 120. It was actually designed by Hadrian himself. The most striking thing about the Pantheon is not its size, immense though it is (until 1960 the dome was the largest ever built); rather it is the remarkable unity of the building. You don't have to look far to find the reason for this harmony: The diameter of the dome is exactly equal to the height of the walls. The hole in the ceiling is intentional: The oculus at the apex of the dome signifies the "all-seeing eye of heaven." Note the original bronze doors: They have survived more than 1,800 years, centuries more than the interior's rich gold ornamentation, long since plundered by popes and emperors. ✉ *Piazza della Rotonda,* ☎ *06/6830–0230.* 🎫 *Free.* ☉ *Mon.–Sat. 9–4:30, Sun. 9–1.*

NEED A
BREAK?

The café scene in the square in front of the Pantheon rivals that of nearby Piazza Navona. The area is ice-cream heaven, with some of Rome's best *gelaterie* within a few steps of one another. Romans consider nearby **Giolitti** (✉ Via Uffizi del Vicario 40) superlative and take the counter by storm. Remember to pay the cashier first and hand the stub to the man at the counter when you order your cone. Giolitti has a good snack counter, too. The shop is closed Monday. If you're a cappuccino addict, head for the nearby **Tazza d'Oro** (⊠ Via degli Orfani 84).

★ ☺ ❼ **Piazza Navona.** This famed 17th-century piazza, which traces the oval form of Emperor Domitian's stadium, is one of Rome's showpiece attractions. It still has the carefree air of the days when it was the scene of Roman circus games, medieval jousts, and 17th-century carnivals. Today, this ravishing setting often attracts fashion photographers and Romans out for their evening *passeggiata* (promenade). The Christmas fair held in the piazza from early December through January 6 is lively and fun for children, with rides, games, Santa Claus and the Befana (the ugly but good witch who brings candy and toys to Italian children on the Epiphany). Bernini's splashing **Fountain of the Four Rivers,** with an enormous rock squared off by statues representing the four corners of the world, makes a fitting centerpiece. Behind the fountain stands the church of **Sant'Agnese in Agone,** the absolute quintessence of Baroque architecture, built by the Pamphili Pope Innocent X and still owned by his descendants, the Princes Doria-Pamphili. The facade— a wonderfully rich melange of bell towers, concave spaces, and dovetailed stone and marble—is by Carlo Rainaldi and Francesco Borromini (1599–1667), a contemporary and sometime rival of Bernini. One story has it that the Bernini statue nearest the church is hiding its head because it can't bear to look upon the "inferior" Borromini facade; in fact, the facade was built after the fountain, and the statue hides its head because it represents the Nile River, whose source was unknown until relatively recently.

NEED A BREAK? The sidewalk tables of the **Tre Scalini** (⊠ Piazza Navona 30) café offer a grandstand view of the piazza. This is the place that invented the *tartufo,* a luscious chocolate-covered ice-cream specialty. Note that it costs twice as much if you eat it outside as inside. The café is closed Wednesday. For a salad or a light lunch, go to **Cul de Sac** (⊠ Piazza Pasquino 73 off Piazza Navona) or to **Insalata Ricca**

(✉ Via del Paradiso next to church of Sant'Andrea della Valle). Both are informal and inexpensive.

❹ San Luigi dei Francesi. Art lovers will want to make a pilgrimage to this church. In the last chapel on the left are three stunningly dramatic works by Caravaggio (1571–1610), the master of the heightened approach to light and dark. The inevitable coin machine will light up his *Calling of St. Matthew, Matthew and the Angel,* and *Matthew's Martyrdom,* seen from left to right, and Caravaggio's mastery of light takes it from there. Time has fully vindicated the artist's patron, Cardinal Francesco del Monte, who commissioned these works and stoutly defended their worth from the consternation of the clergy of San Luigi, who didn't appreciate the artist's roistering and unruly lifestyle; they are now acknowledged as among the world's greatest paintings. ✉ *Piazza San Luigi dei Francesi.* ☉ *Fri.–Wed. 7:30–12:30 and 3:30–7, Thurs. 7:30–12:30.*

❺ Sant'Agostino. Caravaggio's celebrated *Madonna of the Pilgrims*—which scandalized all Rome because it pictured pilgrims with dirt on the soles of their feet—can be found in this small church, over the first altar on the left. ✉ *Piazza di Sant'Agostino.*

⓮ Sant'Andrea della Valle. This huge, 17th-century church looms mightily over a busy intersection. Puccini set the first act of his opera *Tosca* here. Puccini lovers have been known to hire a horse-drawn carriage at night for an evocative journey that traces the course of the opera (from Sant'Andrea up Via Giulia to Palazzo Farnese—Scarpia's headquarters—to the locale of the opera's climax, Castel Sant'Angelo, landmarks that define this part of Rome). ✉ *Piazza Vidoni 6.*

⓯ Sant'Ivo alla Sapienza. Borromini's inspirational church has what must surely be the most fascinating dome in all Rome—a golden spiral said to have been inspired by a bee's stinger. ✉ *Corso Rinascimento 40.*

❽ Santa Maria della Pace. Hidden away in a corner of Old Rome, gracing Piazza Santa Maria della Pace, are a semicircular portico and 15th-century church. In 1656, Pietro da Cortona was commissioned by Pope Alexander VII to enlarge its tiny piazza (to accommodate the carriages of the church's wealthy parishioners), and the result was one of Rome's most delightful little architectural stage sets, complete with bijou-size palaces. Within the church are two great Renaissance treasures: Raphael's frescoes of the Sibyls (above the first altar on the right near the front door) and the cloister designed by Bramante, the very first expression of High Renaissance style in Rome. Santa Maria della Pace is rarely open, but if you take the alleylike Vicolo along the left-hand side of the church and ring the bell at the first entryway on the right, the nuns will usually permit you to enter.

2   **Santa Maria sopra Minerva.** Practically the only Gothic-style church in Rome, the attractions are Michelangelo's *Risen Christ* and the tomb of the gentle 15th-century artist Fra Angelico. Have some coins handy for the *luce* (light) boxes that illuminate the **Carafa Chapel** in the right transept, where exquisite 15th-century frescoes by Filippo Lippi (circa 1457–1504) are well worth the small investment (Lippi's most famous student was Botticelli). In front of the church, Bernini's charming elephant bearing an Egyptian obelisk has an inscription on the base stating something to the effect that it takes a strong mind to sustain solid wisdom. ✉ *Piazza della Minerva.*

Via Giulia was named after its builder, Pope Julius II (of Sistine Ceiling fame), and it has functioned for more than four centuries as the "salon of Rome," address of choice for Roman aristocrats. It is lined with elegant palaces, including Palazzo Falconieri (☞ *above*), and old churches (one, San Eligio, reputedly designed by Raphael himself). The area around Via Giulia is a wonderful section to wander through and get the feel of daily life as carried on in a centuries-old setting; this experience is enhanced by the dozens of antiques shops in the neighborhood.

Vistas and Views: From the Spanish Steps to the Trevi Fountain

Though it has a bustling commercial air, this part of the city also holds some great scenic attractions. The most extravagant of all is the elaborate marble confection that is the monument to Vittorio Emanuele II. Among the things to look for are stately palaces, Baroque ballrooms, and the greatest example of portraiture in Rome, Velazquez's incomparable *Innocent X*. Those with a taste for the sumptuous theatricality of Roman ecclesiastical architecture, and in particular for heroic illusionistic ceiling painting, will find this a rewarding area. But for most, the highlights are the Trevi Fountain and the Spanish Steps, 18th-century Rome's most famous example of city planning.

A Good Walk

Numbers in the text correspond to numbers in the margin and on the Rome map.

Start at the flamboyant **Vittorio Emanuele Monument** ⑮ in Piazza Venezia, home of the **Tomb of the Unknown Soldier.** As you look up the Corso bearing the king's name, to your left is **Palazzo Venezia** ⑯, an art-laden Renaissance palace where Mussolini once addressed the crowds. On Saturdays, you can visit the picture gallery known as **Galleria Colonna**, in the **Palazzo Colonna** ⑰, home to Rome's most patrician family. Along Via del Corso, one of the busiest shopping streets in the city, is the **Palazzo Doria Pamphili** ⑱. A detour to the left will bring you to the sumptuous 17th-century church of **Sant'Ignazio** ⑲. If you continue straight along the Corso you will reach Piazza Colonna and the ancient **Column of Marcus Aurelius** ⑳. Take a left onto chic Via Condotti, which gives you a head-on view of the Piazza di Spagna and the **Spanish Steps** ㉑; on the right of the steps, at No. 26, is the **Keats and Shelley Memorial House** ㉒, in which the English Romantic poet Keats lived. Don't forget to debouch slightly onto Via Gregoriana to discover the **Palazzetto Zuccari** ㉓, designed to look like a grimacing monster. From the narrow end of the piazza, take Via Propaganda Fide to Sant'Andrea delle Fratte, swerving onto Via del Nazareno, then crossing busy Via del Tritone to Via della Stamperia. This street leads to the **Trevi Fountain** ㉔, one of Rome's most familiar landmarks.

TIMING

The walk takes approximately two to three hours. In the morning the air is cleaner and car and pedestrian traffic is lighter.

Sights to See

Numbers in the margin correspond to points of interest on the Rome map.

㉒ Column of Marcus Aurelius. This ancient column is an extraordinary stone history book. Its marvelously detailed reliefs spiraling up to the top relate the emperor's victorious campaigns against the barbarians. ⊠ *Piazza Colonna.*

NEED A BREAK?   The **Antico Caffè Greco,** a 200-year-old institution, ever a haunt of artists and literati, has tiny, marble-top tables and velour settees; it's a beautifully preserved place. Goethe, Byron, and Liszt were habitueés; Buffalo Bill stopped in when his Wild West road show hit Rome. It's still a haven for writers and artists, and for ladies carrying Versace shopping bags. You pay a premium for table service. ⊠ *Via Condotti 86. Closed Sun.*

㉒ Keats and Shelley Memorial House. English Romantic poet Keats lived next to the Spanish Steps in what is now a museum dedicated to himself and his great contemporary and friend, Shelley. You can visit his tiny rooms, which have been poignantly preserved as they were when he died here in 1821. ⊠ *Piazza di Spagna 26,* ☎ *06/678–4235.* ☞ *5,000 lire.* ☉ *June–Sept., weekdays 9–1 and 3–6; Oct.–May, weekdays 9–1 and 2:30–5:30.*

㉓ Palazzetto Zuccari. Near the top of the Spanish Steps (☞ *below*) stands what many consider the most amusing house in all of Italy, at Via Gregoriana 30, designed to look like a grimacing stone monster. The entrance is through the monster's mouth; the eyes are the house's windows. It was designed in 1591 by the Mannerist painter Federico Zuccari (1540–1609), whose home this was. Zuccari sank all his money into this bizarre creation, dying in debt before his curious memorial, as it turned out to be, was completed. It is now the property of the **Biblioteca Hertziana,** Rome's prestigious fine arts library. ⊠ *Via Gregoriana 30.*

㉗ Palazzo Colonna. Rome's most patrician family opens up its fabulous home to the public once a week, and the invitation is irresistible to anyone who ever wondered what a palace looks like inside. The entrance to the picture gallery,

Galleria Colonna, which is open only on Saturday mornings, is a secondary one, behind a plain, obscure-seeming door. The old masters are lackluster, but the gallery should be on your must-do list because the Sala Grande is truly the grandest 17th-century room in Rome. More than 300 feet long, and decorated with a bedazzlement of chandeliers, colored marble, and enormous paintings, it is best known today as the site where Audrey Hepburn met the press in *Roman Holiday.* ✉ *Via della Pilotta 17,* ☎ *06/679–4362.* ✇ *10,000 lire.* ⊙ *Sept.–July, Sat. 9–1.*

⑱ Palazzo Doria Pamphili. The graceful 18th-century facade of this palazzo on Via del Corso is only a small part of a bona-fide patrician palace, still the residence of a princely family, who rent out many of the palazzo's 1,000 rooms. You shouldn't miss seeing the family's incredibly rich art collection, open to the public a few mornings a week. Pride of place is given to the famous (and pitiless) 17th-century Velazquez portrait of the Pamphili Pope Innocent X, but don't overlook Caravaggio's poignant *Rest on the Flight to Egypt*—and, time permitting, catch the guided tour of the state apartments, which gives a discreet glimpse of an aristocratic lifestyle. Pundits say most Roman palazzi consist of one bathroom, two bedrooms, and 40 ballrooms, and after this tour, you can understand why. ✉ *Piazza del Collegio Romano 1/a,* ☎ *06/679–7323.* ✇ *Picture gallery 10,000 lire, private-apartments tour 5,000 lire.* ⊙ *Mon., Tues., and Fri.–Sun. 10–1.*

⑯ Palazzo Venezia. This building is a blend of medieval solidity and Renaissance grace. It offers a unique chance to see what a Renaissance palace really looked like and contains a good collection of paintings, sculptures, and objets d'art in grand salons, some of which Mussolini used as his offices. Notice the balcony over the main portal, from which Il Duce addressed huge crowds in the eponymous
Ⓒ **Piazza Venezia** below. Nowadays, the square's most imposing figure is the policeman directing traffic from his little podium in the middle, whose almost comical display of orchestration is a constant source of amusement to passersby. ✉ *Via del Plebiscito 118,* ☎ *06/679–8865.* ✇ *8,000 lire.* ⊙ *Tues.–Sat. 9–1:30, Sun. 9–12:30.*

⑲ Sant'Ignazio. The false interior dome in this sumptuous 17th-century church is an oddity among the lavishly frescoed domes of the Eternal City. To get the full effect of the marvelous illusionistic ceiling painted by Andrea del Pozzo, stand on the small disk set into the floor of the nave to view his *Glory of St. Ignatius Loyola.* The church contains some of Rome's most splendorous, jewel-encrusted altars. If you're lucky, you might be able to catch one of the evening concerts offered here. The church is the focus of Raguzzini's 18th-century Rococo piazza, where the buildings are arranged almost as in a stage set, reminding us that theatricality was a key element of almost all the best Baroque and Rococo art. ⊠ *Piazza Sant'Ignazio.*

★ ㉑ Spanish Steps. Both the steps and the **Piazza di Spagna,** from which the steps emerge, get their names from the Spanish Embassy to the Holy See (the Vatican), opposite the American Express office, though the staircase was built with French funds in 1723. In an allusion to the Church of Trinità dei Monti at the top of the hill, the staircase is divided by three landings (beautifully banked with blooming azaleas from mid-April to mid-May). For centuries, the Scalinata (as natives refer to the steps) has been the place to see and be seen. This area has always welcomed tourists: 18th-century dukes and duchesses on their Grand Tour, 19th-century artists and writers in search of inspiration—among them, Stendhal, Balzac, Thackeray, and Byron—and today's enthusiastic hordes. Bernini's **Fountain of the Barcaccia** (Old Boat) is near the center of the piazza.

NEED A BREAK? **Babington's Tea Rooms** (⊠ Piazza di Spagna 23), at the foot of the Spanish Steps, has catered to the refined cravings of Anglo-Saxon travelers since its establishment by two genteel English ladies in 1896, but it's definitely not a budgeter's cup of tea. At weekday lunches you're likely to find yourself next to a Bulgari, Fendi, or Agnelli. The restaurant is closed Monday.

★ ㉔ Trevi Fountain. The Colosseum's rival as the sight everyone wants to see in Rome, after St. Peter's, is tucked away off Via del Tritone. The fountain, all the more effective for its cramped setting in a tiny piazza, is a spectacular fantasy of mythical sea creatures amid cascades of splashing waters. It was featured in the 1954 film *Three Coins in the Fountain* and, of course, was the scene of Anita Ekberg's aquatic frolic in Fellini's *La Dolce Vita*. The fountain is the world's most spectacular wishing well: Legend has it that you can ensure your return to Rome by tossing a coin into the fountain. At night, the spotlit piazza takes on the festive air of a crowded outdoor party.

⑮ **Vittorio Emanuele Monument.** The huge bronze sculpture group atop this vast marble monument is visible from many parts of the city, making this modern Rome's most flamboyant landmark. It was erected in the late 19th century to honor Italy's first king, Vittorio Emanuele II, and the unification of Italy. Sometimes said to resemble a typewriter in the Victorian mode, it houses the **Tomb of the Unknown Soldier,** with its eternal flame. Although the monument has been closed to the public for many years, plans are in the works to reopen it; the views from the top of the steps are among Rome's best, because for one thing, the monument isn't in it. Opposite the monument, note the enclosed wooden veranda fronting the palace on the corner of Via del Plebiscito and the Corso. For the many years that she lived in Rome, Napoléon's mother had a fine view from here of the local goings-on. ⊠ *Piazza Venezia.*

Historic Churches: Heavenly Monuments of Faith

It is hard not to be impressed by the historic and architectural grandeur of Rome's major churches. Three churches are the highlights of this walk, two of them major basilicas with roots in the early centuries of Christianity.

A Good Walk

Not far from Piazza Venezia and the Roman Forum, off Via Cavour is the church of **San Pietro in Vincoli** ㉕. Look for Via San Francesco da Paola, a street staircase that passes under the old Borgia palace and leads to the church. Via Cavour leads to **Santa Maria Maggiore** ㉖, and from there Via Merulana leads straight to **San Giovanni in Laterano** ㉗. The adjoining **Lateran Palace** houses the Vatican Historical Museum; across the street, a small building houses the **Scala Santa** ㉘, or Holy Stairs, supposedly from Pilate's Jerusalem palace. Circle the palace to see the 6th-century octagonal **Baptistery of San Giovanni,** forerunner of many such buildings throughout Italy.

TIMING

The walk alone takes approximately 90 minutes, plus 15–20 minutes in the churches. Allow at least an hour to explore San Clemente. The visit to the Vatican Historical Museum takes about 45 minutes.

Sights to See

㉗ **San Giovanni in Laterano.** Many are surprised when they discover that the cathderal of Rome is not St. Peter's but this church. Dominating the piazza whose name it shares, this immense building was where the early popes once lived and where the present pope still officiates in his capacity as Rome's bishop. The towering facade and Borromini's cool Baroque interior emphasize the majesty of its proportions.

The adjoining **Lateran Palace,** once the popes' official residence and still technically part of the Vatican, now houses the offices of the Rome Diocese and the Vatican Historical Museum. ▨ *6,000 lire.* ⊘ *museum Sat. and the first Sun. of each month 8:45–1.*

OFF THE
BEATEN
PATH

SAN CLEMENTE – The remains of ancient Roman dwellings and a 4th-century church below the upper church of San Clemente are among Rome's most intriguing subterranean sights. ⊠ *Via San Giovanni in Laterano,* ☎ *06/704-51018.* ▨ *Donation requested.* ⊘ *Mon.–Sat. 9–noon and 3:30–6, Sun. 10–noon.*

SANTI QUATTRO CORONATI – This 12th-century church, part of a fortified abbey that provided refuge to early popes and emperors, is in one of the most unusual corners of Rome, a quiet island that has resisted the tide of time and traffic flowing beneath its ramparts. Few places in Rome are as redolent of the Middle Ages. Don't miss the cloister with its well-tended gardens and 12th-century fountain. The entrance is the door in the left nave; ring if it's not open. You can also ring at the adjacent convent for the key to the Oratory of San Silvestro, with charming 13th-century frescoes.

㉖ **Santa Maria Maggiore.** One of the oldest and most spacious churches in Rome, it was built on the spot where a 3rd-century pope witnessed a miraculous midsummer snowfall. It is resplendent with gleaming mosaics—those on the arch in front of the main altar date from the 5th century; the apse mosaic dates from the 13th century—and an opulently carved wood ceiling believed to have been gilded with the first gold brought from the New World. ⌧ *Piazza Santa Maria Maggiore off Via Cavour.*

㉕ The church of **San Pietro in Vincoli** houses St. Peter's chains (under the altar) and Michelangelo's *Moses,* a powerful statue almost as famed as his frescoes in the Sistine Chapel. The *Moses* was destined for the tomb of Julius II, but Michelangelo was driven to distraction by the interference of Pope Julius and his successors, and the tomb was never finished. The statue is a remarkable sculpture but the church is usually jammed with tour groups, and the monument itself fronts a large, ugly souvenir shop. ⌧ *Piazza San Pietro in Vincoli off Via Cavour.*

㉘ **Scala Santa.** A small building opposite the Lateran Palace (☞ *above*) houses the so-called Holy Stairs, claimed to be the staircase from Pilate's palace in Jerusalem. Behind the palace is the 6th-century octagonal **Baptistery of San Giovanni,** forerunner of many similar buildings throughout Italy, and Rome's oldest and tallest obelisk, brought from Thebes and dating from the 15th century BC.

From the Quirinale to the Piazza della Repubblica: Princely Palaces and Romantic Fountains

Although this walk takes you from ancient Roman sculptures to early Christian churches, it's mainly an excursion into the 16th and 17th centuries, when Baroque art—and Bernini—triumphed in Rome.

A Good Walk

Begin at the **Quirinal** ㉙, the highest of Rome's seven hills. Here you'll find the Palazzo del Quirinale, official residence of the president of Italy. Also of note is the **Palazzo Pallavicini-Rospigliosi** ㉚, a 17th-century palace with some exquisite examples of Baroque art. Along Via del Quirinal (which becomes Via XX Settembre) is the church of **Sant'-Andrea** ㉛, considered by many to be Bernini's finest work, and, at the Quattro Fontane (Four Fountains) crossroads, the church of **San Carlo alle Quattro Fontane** ㉜, designed by Bernini's rival Borromini. Turn left down Via delle Quattro Fontane to reach the imposing Palazzo Barberini, home of the **Galleria Nazionale** ㉝, home to splendid masterpieces by Raphael and Caravaggio. Down the hill is Piazza Barberini and the **Tritone Fountain** ㉞, another Bernini design. Cross the piazza and begin your gradual climb up Via Veneto, curving past the U.S. Embassy and turning off onto Via Bissolati. On the corner of Piazza San Bernardo is the church of **Santa Maria della Vittoria** ㊱, known for Bernini's Baroque decoration. It's not far to **Piazza della Repubblica** ㊲, where you will find the pretty **Fountain of the Naiads.** On one side of the square is an ancient Roman brick facade, which marks the church of Santa Maria degli Angeli. On the opposite side of the square is the last stop on this walk, the **Museo Nazionale Romano** ㊳, where there are plentiful examples of the fine mosaics and masterful paintings that decorated ancient Rome's villas and palaces.

TIMING

The walk takes approximately 90 minutes, plus 10–15 minutes for each church visited, and two hours each for visits to the Galleria Nazionale in Palazzo Barberini and the Museo Nazionale Romano.

Sights to See

❸❸ **Galleria Nazionale.** Along with architect Carlo Maderno, Borromini helped make the splendid 17th-century Palazzo Barberini a residence worthy of Rome's leading art patron, Pope Urban VIII, who began this palazzo for his family in 1625. Inside, the gallery offers some fine works by Raphael (the *Fornarina*) and by Caravaggio. The palazzo boasts Rome's biggest ballroom, which has a ceiling painted by Pietro da Cortona; this shows Immortality bestowing a crown upon Divine Providence escorted by—"a bomber squadron," to quote Sir Michael Levey—of mutant bees (bees featured prominently in the heraldic device of the Barberini). ⊠ *Via delle Quattro Fontane 13,* ☎ *06/481–4591.* 🎫 *8,000 lire.* ☉ *Tues.–Sat. 9–2, Sun. 9–1.*

③⑧ Museo Nazionale Romano. Palazzo Massimo alle Terme holds a major part of the collections of the National Museum. Here you can see extraordinary examples of the fine mosaics and masterful paintings that decorated ancient Rome's palaces and villas, as well as some of antiquity's most fabled sculptures, including the *Ludovisi Throne,* the *Lancellotti Discus Thrower,* and the *Castelporziano Discus Thrower.* Don't miss the fresco—depicting a lush garden in bloom—which came from the villa that Livia, wife of Emperor Augustus, owned outside Rome. ✉ *Largo Villa Peretti 2,* ☎ *06/489–03501.* ▣ *12,000 lire (includes Terme di Diocleziano museum).* ⊙ *Tues.–Sat. 9–2, Sun. 9–1.*

③⓪ Palazzo Pallavicini-Rospigliosi. This palace was built in 1605 for Cardinal Scipione Borghese; on the first day of each month, visitors can view Guido Reni's fresco of *Aurora*—a landmark in Baroque painting—in the palace's park pavilion. It is just off the square. ✉ *Via XXIV Maggio 43,* ☎ *06/482–7224.* ▣ *Free.* ⊙ *1st day of month 10–noon and 3–5.*

③⑦ Piazza della Repubblica has a characteristic 19th-century layout, but the curving porticoes echo the plan of those portions of the immense ancient **Baths of Diocletian,** which once stood here. Built in the 4th century AD, they were the largest and most impressive of the baths of ancient Rome, and their vast halls, pools, and gardens could accommodate 3,000 people at a time. Also part of the great baths was an **Octagonal Hall,** which now holds a sampling of ancient sculptures found there, including two beautiful bronzes. ✉ *Via Romita.* ▣ *Free.* ⊙ *Daily 9–1 and 3–6.*

Another part of the Baths of Diocletian was later transformed into a monastery and then into the **Terme di Diocleziano Museum,** holding the Museo Nazionale Romano's collection of ancient inscriptions on stone, interesting to the average visitor mainly as a chance to see the lovely cloister, with bits and pieces of ancient Rome lining the garden paths. ✉ *Viale E. De Nicola 79,* ☎ *06/488–0530.* ▣ *12,000 lire (includes Palazzo Massimo alle Terme).* ⊙ *Tues.–Sat. 9–2, Sun. 9–1.*

The pretty **Fountain of the Naiads,** a turn-of-the-century addition to the piazza, features voluptuous bronze ladies wrestling happily with marine monsters. The curving ancient Roman brick facade on one side of the piazza marks the church of **Santa Maria degli Angeli,** adapted by Michelangelo from the vast central chamber of the colossal baths. The scale of the church's interior gives you an idea of the grandeur of the ancient building.

㉙ Quirinal. This is the highest of ancient Rome's seven hills (the others are the Capitoline, Palatine, Esquiline, Viminal, Celian, and Aventine) and the one where ancient Romans and, later, the popes built their residences in order to escape the deadly miasmas and the malaria of the low-lying area around the Forum. Every day at 4 PM the ceremony of the changing of the guards at the portal includes a sprightly mini-parade, complete with band. The fountain in the square boasts ancient statues of Castor and Pollux reining in their unruly steeds, and a basin salvaged from the Roman Forum. The **Palazzo del Quirinale,** the largest on the Quirinal square, belonged first to the popes, then to Italy's kings, and is now the official residence of the nation's president.

㉜ San Carlo alle Quattro Fontane. Borromini's church at the Quattro Fontane (Four Fountains) crossroads is an architectural gem. In a space no larger than the base of one of the piers of St. Peter's, Borromini created a church that is an intricate exercise in geometric perfection. Characteristically, the architect chose a subdued white stucco for the interior decoration, so as not to distract from the form. The exterior of the church is Borromini at his bizarre best, all curves and rippling movement. Outside, four charming fountains frame views in four directions.

㉟ Santa Maria della Concezione. One of the most bizarre sights in Rome is the crypt of this Capuchin church, where you can see—if you like that sort of thing—the skeletons and assorted bones of 4,000 dead monks artistically arranged in four macabre chapels. ⊠ *Via Veneto 27,* ☎ *06/ 487–1185.* ▣ *Donation requested.* ☉ *Daily 9–noon and 3–6.*

㊱ Santa Maria della Vittoria. This church in Via XX Settembre is known for Bernini's Baroque decoration of the Cornaro Chapel, an exceptional fusion of architecture, painting, and sculpture, in which the *Ecstasy of St. Teresa* is the focal point. Bernini's audacious conceit was to model the chapel as a theater: Members of the Cornaro family—sculpted in colored marble—watch from theater boxes as, center stage, St. Teresa, in the throes of mystical rapture, is pierced by a gilded arrow held by an angel. To quote one 18th-century observer, President de Brosses: "If that is divine love, I know what it is." No matter what your reaction may be, you'll have to admit it's great theater.

③ **Sant'Andrea.** This is a small but imposing Baroque church designed and decorated by Bernini, who considered it one of his finest works and liked to come here occasionally just to sit and enjoy it. ⊠ *Via del Quirinale.*

④ **Tritone Fountain.** Centerpiece of Piazza Barberini is Bernini's graceful fountain, designed in 1637 for the sculptor's munificent patron, Pope Urban VIII, whose Barberini coat of arms, featuring bees once again, is at the base of the large shell.

NEED A BREAK?   Next to a movie house, **La Piazza** (⊠ Via Barberini 19) offers the Italian version of fast food, tasty and inexpensive. The restaurant is closed Sunday.

Amid Sylvan Glades: From the Villa Borghese to the Ara Pacis

Beautiful masterpieces are as common as bricks on this walk, which offers more visual excitement than most cities possess in their entire environs. Along the way, Villa Borghese, Rome's largest park, can prevent gallery gout by offering an oasis in which to enjoy an espresso at the Casino Valadier or picnic under the ilex trees. Just be sure to pick up your foodstuffs in advance, whether ready-to-go from the snack bars or do-it-yourself from *alimentari* (grocery stores), as you'll find only fast-food carts within the park itself.

A Good Walk

Start at **Porta Pinciana** ㊴, one of the entrances to Rome's largest park, Villa Borghese. Taking a looping route through the park you will come upon the **Galleria Borghese** ㊵ and its fabulous sculpture collection. Enjoy the view of Rome from the **Pincio** ㊶ terrace, in the southwest corner of the

park, before descending the ramps to **Piazza del Popolo** ㊷.
At the north end of the piazza, next to the 400-year-old city
gate, the Porta del Popolo, is the church of **Santa Maria del
Popolo** ㊸, with one of the richest art collections of any
church in the city. Stroll along Via Ripetta to the Augusteum, built by Caesar Augustus; next to it is the **Ara Pacis** ㊹,
built in 13 BC.

TIMING

The walk takes approximately two hours; allow an additional hour for the Galleria Borghese and 20–30 minutes
for the Augusteum.

Sights to See

㊹ **Ara Pacis (Altar of Augustan Peace).** This altar, sheltered in
an unattractive modern edifice on the northwest corner of
Piazza Augusto Imperatore, was erected in 13 BC to celebrate
the era of peace ushered in by Augustus's military victories.
The reliefs showing the procession of the Roman imperial
family are magnificent and moving. Notice the poignant presence of several forlorn children; historians now believe they
attest to the ambition of Augustus's wife, the Empress Livia,
who succeeded in having her son, Tiberius, ascend to the
throne by dispatching his family rivals with poison. Next
to it is the imposing bulk of the marble-clad **mausoleum** Augustus built for himself and his family. ✉ *Mausoleum: Via
Ripetta,* ☎ *06/671–0271.* 🎟 *3,750 lire.* ☉ *May–Sept.,
Wed.–Fri. 9–1:30; Tues., Thurs., and Sat. 9–1:30 and 4–
7; Sun. 9–1. Oct.–Apr., Tues.–Sat. 9–1:30, Sun. 9–1.*

㊵ **Galleria Borghese** was a pleasure palace created by Cardinal Scipione Borghese in 1613 as a showcase for his fabulous antiquities collection and elegant fetes. Today, it's a
monument to Roman 18th-century interior decoration at
its most extravagant: room after room opulently adorned
with porphyry and alabaster. Throughout the grand salons
are statues of various deities, including one officially known
as Venus Vincitrix, but there has never been any doubt as
to its real subject: Pauline Bonaparte, Napoléon's sister, who
married Prince Camillo Borghese in one of the storied
matches of the 19th century. Sculpted by Canova, the
princess reclines on a chaise longue, bare-bosomed, her hips
swathed in classical drapery, the very model of haughty de-

tachment and sly come-hither. Pauline is known to have been shocked that her husband took pleasure in showing off the work to his guests. This coyness seems all the more curious given the reply she is supposed to have made to a lady who asked her how she could have posed for the work: "Oh, but the studio was heated." But then it was exactly the combination of aristocratic disdain and naïveté that is said to have made her irresistible in the first place. Other rooms at the Galleria Borghese hold important sculptures by Bernini, including the *David* and *Apollo and Daphne*. The gallery's renowned picture collection has been moved to the large San Francesco a Ripa complex in Trastevere; it will probably be there through 1997 (☞ Across the Tiber, *below*). ✉ *During renovation, use Galleria Borghese entrance off Via Raimondi,* ☎ *06/854–8577.* 🎟 *4,000 lire.* ⊙ *May–Sept., Tues.–Sat. 9–7, Sun. 9–1; Oct.–Apr., Tues.–Sun. 9–1.*

㊷ Piazza del Popolo. For many years this beautifully proportioned square functioned as an exceptionally attractive parking lot that happened to have a 3,000-year-old obelisk in the middle (now traffic and parking are limited). The often-photographed bookend Baroque churches at the southern end of the piazza are not, first appearances to the contrary, twins. At one end of the square is the 400-year-old **Porta del Popolo,** Rome's northern city gate.

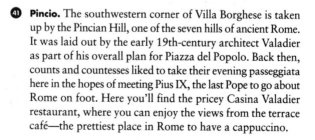

NEED A   **Rosati** (✉ Piazza del Popolo 4) is a café that has never
BREAK?   gone out of style, forever a rendezvous of literati, artists, and actors. Its sidewalk tables, tearoom, and upstairs dining room can revive you with an espresso, snack, lunch, or dinner—all with a hefty price tag.

㊶ Pincio. The southwestern corner of Villa Borghese is taken up by the Pincian Hill, one of the seven hills of ancient Rome. It was laid out by the early 19th-century architect Valadier as part of his overall plan for Piazza del Popolo. Back then, counts and countesses liked to take their evening passeggiata here in the hopes of meeting Pius IX, the last Pope to go about Rome on foot. Here you'll find the pricey Casina Valadier restaurant, where you can enjoy the views from the terrace café—the prettiest place in Rome to have a cappuccino.

③⑨ The **Porta Pinciana** (Pincian Gate) is one of the historic city gates in the Aurelian Walls surrounding Rome. The Porta itself was built in the 6th century AD, about three centuries after the walls were built to keep out the barbarians. These

↻ days it is one of the entrances to **Villa Borghese,** Rome's peaceful 17th-century park, built as the pleasure gardens of the powerful Borghese family.

④③ **Santa Maria del Popolo.** This church next to the Porta del Popolo (☞ *above*) goes almost unnoticed, but it has one of the richest collections of art of any church in Rome. Here you'll find Raphael's High Renaissance masterpiece, the Chigi Chapel, as well as two stunning Caravaggios in the Cerasi Chapel, which definitively prove just how modern 17th-century art can be. Elsewhere in the church, the great names—Bramante, Bernini, Pinturicchio, Sansovino, Caracci—resound in the silence. ✉ *Piazza del Popolo.*

Across the Tiber: The Ghetto, Tiber Island, and Trastevere

For the authentic atmosphere of old Rome, the areas covered in this walk are unbeatable. It takes you through separate communities, each staunchly resisting the tides of change, including the Jewish ghetto; and the Trastevere, a picturesque neighborhood, where you will find "the Romans of Rome": blunt, uninhibited, sharp-eyed, friendly, sincere, often beautiful, and seldom varnished. Despite rampant gentrification, Trastevere remains about the most tightly knit community in Rome, its inhabitants proudly proclaiming their descent—whether real or imagined—from the ancient Romans.

A Good Walk

Begin in the old ghetto, on Via del Teatro Marcello. Turn into Piazza Campitelli and make your way to Piazza Mattei, where one of Rome's loveliest fountains, the 16th-century **Fontana delle Tartarughe** ㊺, is tucked away. Take Via della Reginella into **Via Portico d'Ottavia,** heart of the Jewish ghetto. On the Tiber is a **synagogue.** The **Teatro di Marcello** ㊻, behind the **Portico d'Ottavio,** was originally a theater designed to hold 20,000 people. Follow Via di Teatro di Marcello, passing the ruins of two small temples: the **Temple of Fortuna Virilis** ㊼ and the circular **Temple of Vesta** ㊽. From there, follow the Tiber to **Piazza Bocca della Verità**㊾, home to the marble "mouth of truth" set into the entry portico of the 12th-century **Santa Maria in Cosmedin.** Retracing your steps, cross **Tiberina Island** ㊿, and then head into **Trastevere.** Begin your exploration of the neighborhood at **Piazza in Piscinula** (you will need a good street map to make your way around this intricate maze of winding side streets), take Via dell'Arco dei Tolomei, cross Via dei Salumi, and turn left into Via dei Genovesi and then right to the piazza in front of **Santa Cecilia in Trastevere** ㉛. Aficionados of the Baroque will want to walk several blocks down Via Anicia to **San Francesco a Ripa** ㉜, another Bernini creation. Follow Via San Francesco a Ripa to the very heart of the *rione,* or district, of Trastevere, to the lovely **Piazza di Santa Maria in Trastevere** ㉝, site of the 12th-century church of **Santa Maria in Trastevere.** With the help of a map, find your way through the narrow byways to Piazza Sant'Egidio and Via della Scala, continuing on to Via della Lungara, where you'll find **Villa Farnesina** ㉞, which includes frescoes by Raphael. From Trastevere, climb Via Garibaldi to the Janiculum Hill, which offers views spanning the whole city, and where you'll find the church of **San Pietro in Montorio** ㉟, built in 1481.

TIMING

The walk takes approximately 3 hours, plus 10–15 minutes for each church visited, and about 30 minutes for a visit to Villa Farnesina.

Sights to See

㊺ **Fontana della Tartarughe.** The 16th-century "Fountain of the Turtles" in Piazza Mattei is one of Rome's loveliest. Designed by Giacomo della Porta in 1581 and sculpted by Taddeo Landini, the piece revolves around four bronze boys, each grasping a dolphin that jets water into marble shells, and several bronze tortoises each held in the boys' hands and drinking from the fountain's upper basin. The tortoises are the fountain's most brilliant feature, a 17th-century addition by, inevitably, Bernini. The piazza is named for the Mattei family, which built **Palazzo Mattei** on Via Caetani, worth a peek for its sculpture-rich courtyard and staircase.

Palazzo Corsini. This elegant palace holds a collection of large, dark, and dull paintings, but stop in to climb the extraordinary 17th-century stone staircase, itself a drama of architectural shadows and sculptural voids. ✉ *Via della Lungara 10.*

㊾ Piazza Bocca della Verità—the Square of the Mouth of Truth— is on the site of the Forum Boarium, ancient Rome's cattle market, later used for public executions. Its sinister name is derived from the marble mouth—actually part of an ancient drain cover—set into the entry portico of the 12th-century church of **Santa Maria in Cosmedin.** In the Middle Ages anyone accused of lying would be forced to put his hand into the mouth and warned that if he didn't tell the truth the mouth would close and cut off his hand.

OFF THE
BEATEN
PATH

AVENTINE HILL – One of the seven hills of ancient Rome, it is now a quiet residential neighborhood that most tourists don't see. It has several of the city's oldest and least-visited churches, and some surprises: the view from the keyhole in the gate to the garden of the Knights of Malta (✉ Piazza Cavalieri di Malta) and another, unusual view of Rome from the walled park off Via Santa Sabina.

㊿ Piazza di Santa Maria in Trastevere, with its elegant raised fountain and sidewalk cafés, is a sort of outdoor living room, open to all comers. The showpiece is the 12th-century church of **Santa Maria in Trastevere.** The mosaics on the church's facade—which add light and color to the piazza, especially at night when they are spotlit—are believed to represent the Wise and Foolish Virgins. The interior often produces involuntary gasps from unsuspecting visitors: an enormous nave bathed in a mellow glow from medieval mosaics and overhead gilding, the whole framed by a processional of two rows of gigantic columns. There are larger naves in Rome, but none quite so majestic. Indeed, although it was completed in the 12th century, it approximates—as well as any structure could—the over-the-top splendor of an ancient Roman basilica hall.

㉒ San Francesco a Ripa. This church in Piazza San Francesco d'Assisi is a must for fans of the Baroque. It holds one of Bernini's most hallucinatory sculptures, a dramatically lighted statue of the Blessed Ludovica Albertoni, ecstatic at the prospect of entering heaven as she expires on her deathbed.

(55) **San Pietro in Montorio.** One of the key Renaissance buildings in Rome stands in the cloister of this church, built by order of Ferdinand and Isabella of Spain in 1481 over the spot where tradition says St. Peter was crucified. The **Tempietto,** Bramante's little temple, is an architectural gem, and was one of the earliest and most successful attempts to produce an entirely classical building. ✉ *Via Garibaldi Gianicolo.* ⏲ *Daily 9–12 and 4–6.*

(51) **Santa Cecilia in Trastevere.** Mothers and children love to wander in the delightful little garden in front of this church in Piazza Santa Cecilia, and there's no reason why you shouldn't join them for a bit before you duck inside for a look at the very grand 18th-century interior and the languid statue of St. Cecilia under the altar.

Synagogue. The large, bronze-roofed synagogue on the Tiber is a Roman landmark. It contains an interesting museum of precious ritual objects and fabrics and other exhibits documenting the history of the Jewish community in Rome. ✉ *Lungotevere Cenci,* ☎ *06/686–4648.* 🎟 *8,000 lire.* ⏲ *Mon.–Thurs. 9:30–1:30 and 2–5, Fri. 9:30–2, Sun. 9:30–12:30.*

㊻ **Teatro di Marcello.** The Teatro is hardly recognizable as a theater today, but originally it was a huge place, designed to hold 20,000 spectators. It was begun by Julius Caesar; today, the apartments carved out in its remains have become one of Rome's most prestigious residential addresses. ✉ *Via del Teatro di Marcello.* ⏲ *Only for concerts.*

㊼ **Temple of Fortuna Virilis.** This rectangular temple dates from the 2nd century BC and is built in the Greek style, as was the norm in the early years of Rome. For its age, it is remarkably well-preserved, in part due to its subsequent consecration as a Christian church. ✉ *Piazza Bocca della Verità.*

㊽ **Temple of Vesta.** One of Rome's most evocative little ruins, all but one of its 20 original Corinthian columns remain intact. Like the Temple of Fortuna Virilis (☞ *above*), it was built in the 2nd century BC, considerably before the ruins you see in the Roman Forum. ⊠ *Piazza Bocca dell Verità.*

⑩ Tiberina Island. Ancient Ponte Fabricio links the ghetto neighborhood of Trastevere (☞ *below*) to this island, where a city hospital stands on a site that has been dedicated to healing ever since a temple to Aesculapius was erected here in 291 BC. If you have time, and if the river's not too high, walk down the stairs for a different perspective on the island and the Tiber.

Trastevere. This area consists of a maze of narrow streets that is still, despite evident gentrification, one of the city's most authentically Roman neighborhoods. Literally translated, Trastevere means "across the Tiber," and indeed the Trasteverini, a breed apart, have always been proud and combative, chagrined at the reputation their quarter has acquired for purse snatching (but it happens; don't carry a purse and keep your camera out of sight). Among self-consciously picturesque trattorias and trendy tearooms, you also find old shops and dusty artisans' workshops in alleys festooned with laundry hung out to dry. One of the most unaffected parts of Trastevere lies around **Piazza in Piscinula,** where the tiny **San Benedetto,** the smallest medieval church in the city, is opposite the restored medieval Casa dei Mattei. Via dell'Arco dei Tolomei and Via dei Salumi are interesting old streets.

Via Portico d'Ottavia. Along this street at the heart of the Jewish ghetto are buildings where medieval inscriptions, ancient friezes, and half-buried classical monuments attest to the venerable history of this neighborhood. The old **Church of Sant'Angelo in Pescheria** was built right into the ruins of the Portico d'Ottavia, which served as a kind of foyer for the Teatro di Marcello (☞ *above*).

㊹ Villa Farnesina. Money was no object to extravagant host Agostino Chigi, a banker from Siena who financed many a papal project. His munificence is evident in this elegant villa, built for him in about 1511. When Raphael could steal some precious time from his work on the Vatican Stanze and from his wooing of the Fornarina, he came over to execute some of the frescoes, notably a luminous *Galatea.* Chigi delighted in impressing guests by having his servants clear the table by casting precious dinnerware into the Tiber. Naturally, the guests did not know of the nets he had stretched under the waterline to catch everything. ⊠ *Via della Lungara 230,* ☎ *06/654–0565.* 🎫 *Free.* 🕐 *Mon.–Sat. 9–1.*

Quo Vadis? The Catacombs and the Appian Way

The legendary beginnings of Christianity in Rome are the focus of this tour. Although it offers a respite from museums, the itinerary is no easier on the feet. Do it on a sunny day and take along a picnic or have lunch at one of the pleasant restaurants near the catacombs. The Rome EPT office offers a free, informative pamphlet on this itinerary.

A Good Walk

Resist any temptation to undertake the 1½ km walk between Porta San Sebastiano and the catacombs; it is a dull and tiring hike on a heavily trafficked, cobblestone road, with stone walls the only scenery. Instead, hop on Bus 218 from San Giovanni in Laterano or Bus 660 from the Colli Albani Metro stop on Line A to the **Via Appia Antica** ㊽. Stay on the bus until you reach the catacombs; the most interesting and scenic walk along the ancient road lies beyond them.

TIMING

One hour, plus one hour for visit to catacombs.

Sights to See

㊽ **Via Appia Antica.** This is "the Queen of Roads," completed in 312 BC by Appius Claudius, who also built Rome's first aqueduct. One of the two important catacombs on Via Appia Antica is that of **San Callisto,** one of the best preserved of these underground cemeteries. A friar will guide you through its crypts and galleries. ⊠ *Via Appia Antica 110,* ☎ *06/513–6725.* 🎫 *8,000 lire.* 🕐 *Apr.–Sept., Thurs.–Tues. 8:30–noon and 2:30–5:30; Oct.–Mar., Thurs.–Tues. 8:30–noon and 2:30–5.*

The 4th-century catacomb of **San Sebastiano** was named for the saint who was buried here. It burrows underground on four levels. The only one of the catacombs to remain accessible during the Middle Ages, it is the origin of the term "catacomb," for it was in a spot where the road dips into a hollow, a place the Romans called *catacumbas* (near the hollow). Eventually, the Christian cemetery that had existed here since the 2nd century came to be known by the same name, which was applied to all underground cemeteries discovered in Rome in later centuries. ⊠ *Via Appia Antica 136,* ☎ *06/788–7035.* ⊠ *8,000 lire.* ☉ *Apr.–Sept., Fri.–Wed. 9–noon and 2:30–7:30; Oct.–Mar., Fri.–Wed. 9–noon and 2:30–5.*

On the east side of Via Appia Antica are the ruins of the **Circus of Maxentius,** where the obelisk now in Piazza Navona once stood.

The circular **Tomb of Cecilia Metella,** mausoleum of a Roman noblewoman who lived at the time of Julius Caesar, was transformed into a fortress in the 14th century. It marks the beginning of the most interesting and evocative stretch of Via Appia Antica, lined with tombs and fragments of statuary. Cypresses and umbrella pines stand guard over the ruined sepulchers, and the occasional tracts of ancient paving stones are the same ones trod by triumphant Roman legions.

3 Dining

AS THE PACE OF ROMAN life quickens, more fast-food outlets are opening, offering tourists a wider choice of light meals. There are variations of the older Italian institutions of the *tavola calda* (hot table) and the *rosticceria* (roast meats), both of which offer hot and cold dishes to be taken out or eaten on the premises, some sold by the portion, others by weight. You usually select your food and pay for it at the cashier, who gives you a stub to give to the counter person when you pick up the food. Newer snack bars are cropping up, and pizza *rustica* (rustic-style) outlets selling slices of various kinds of pizza seem to have sprouted on every block.

Despite these changes, many Romans stick to the tradition of having their main meal at lunch, from 1 to 3, although you won't be turned away if hunger strikes shortly after noon. Dinner is served from 8 or 8:30 until about 10:30 or 11. Some restaurants stay open much later, especially in summer, when patrons linger at sidewalk tables to enjoy the *ponentino* (cool breeze). Almost all restaurants close one day a week (it's usually safest to call ahead to reserve) and for at least two weeks in August, when it can sometimes seem impossible to find sustenance in the deserted city. This is not a bad time to picnic. You can buy provisions in neighborhood *alimentari* that aren't closed for vacation.

Generally, a typical meal in a restaurant or trattoria consists of at least two courses: a first course of pasta, risotto, or soup; and a second course of meat or fish. Side dishes such as vegetables and salads cost extra, as do desserts. There is no such thing as a side dish of pasta; pasta is a course in itself and Italians would never think of serving a salad with it; the salad comes later. Now, about antipasto: Many a misunderstanding arises over a lavish offering of antipasto, which literally means "before the meal." No matter how generous and varied the antipasto, the host expects those who have one to order at least one other course. Pizza is in a category by itself and is a one-dish meal, even for the Italians. But some replace the starter course of pasta with a small pizza.

The typical Roman pasta is fettuccine, golden egg noodles that are at their classic best when freshly made and laced with *ragù,* a thick, rich tomato and meat sauce. Carbonara-style pasta is usually made with spaghetti or thicker, spaghetti-like *bucatini;* the cooked pasta is tossed with raw egg, chunks of fried *guanciale* (unsmoked bacon), and lots of freshly ground black pepper. Spaghetti *all'amatriciana* has a piquant sauce of tomato, guanciale, and hot red pepper. Gnocchi, a Roman favorite for Thursday dinner, are tiny dumplings of flour and potatoes and are served with a tomato sauce and a sprinkling of grated cheese.

Abbacchio, baby lamb, is at its best in the spring; a summer favorite is *pollo coi peperoni,* stewed chicken with peppers. *Fritto misto* usually includes morsels of zucchini, artichokes, and *baccalà* (codfish) fried in batter. *Carciofi* (artichokes) are served *alla romana* (sautéed whole with garlic and mint), or *alla giudia* (fried whole, with each petal crisp and light enough to melt in your mouth). Tender peas are sautéed with prosciutto to make *piselli al* prosciutto.

Local cheeses are mild *caciotta* and sharp pecorino. Fresh ricotta is also used in a number of dishes. Typical wines of Rome are those of the Castelli Romani: Frascati, Colli Albani, Marino, and Velletri.

Acqua semplice (tap water) is safe everywhere in Rome, so if you're on a budget, order it rather than *acqua minerale* (mineral water). *Acqua minerale* can be ordered either *gassata* (carbonated) or *naturale,* or *nongassata* (without bubbles) and in *litro* (liter) or *mezzo litro* (half-liter) size. The automatically applied *pane e coperto* (bread and cover charge) has been eliminated in many restaurants but you may be charged extra for bread, anyway. And a *servizio* (service charge) of 10%–12% still appears on many checks; remember that in the end your waiter will see only a small part of that sum, so another 5% is welcome. A fixed-price *menù turistico* (tourist menu) includes taxes and services, but usually not drinks.

CATEGORY	COST*
$$$$	over 120,000 lire
$$$	70,000–120,000 lire
$$	40,000–70,000 lire
$	under 40,000 lire

per person, for a three-course meal, including house wine and taxes

Central Rome

$$$$ ✕ **El Toulà.** Take a byway off Piazza Nicosia in Old Rome to find this prestigious restaurant, one of a number in Italy of the same name; all are spin-offs of a renowned restaurant in Treviso in northern Italy. Rome's El Toulà has the warm, welcoming atmosphere of a 19th-century country house, with white walls, antique furniture in dark wood, heavy silver serving dishes, and spectacular arrangements of fruits and flowers. There's a cozy bar off the entrance, where you can sip a *prosecco* (Venetian semisparkling white wine), the aperitif best suited to the chef's Venetian specialties, which include risotto with artichokes and *fegato alla veneziana* (liver with onions). ⊠ *Via della Lupa 29/b,* ☎ *06/687–3750. Reservations essential. Jacket and tie. AE, DC, MC, V. No lunch Sat. Closed Sun., Aug., and Dec. 24–26.*

$$$$ ✕ **La Pergola.** A grand view. A grand restaurant. The conjunction is not automatic—but in this case, both elements are imposingly present. From this elegant rooftop restaurant of the Cavalieri Hilton—built on Monte Mario, one of the highest of the hills overlooking the city—a fabulous view of Rome whets your appetite for imaginatively prepared cuisine. Wraparound windows and mirrors ensure that everyone gets a panoramic view of the city's skyline. And if you can take your eyes off the vista you will find a distinctively Italian ambience, with frescoes and a Tuscan garden theme featuring lattice-work and potted lemon trees. The menu changes with the seasons, and might include pasta with shrimp and arugula or breast of guinea hen on a red-wine-and-onion confit. Order à la carte or from three special menus, priced at 85,000, 105,000, and 135,000 lire. Then have an after-dinner drink in the adjacent bar and try to spot the constellations in the Roman sky. You may dine outdoors in fair weather. ⊠ *Via Cadlolo 101,* ☎ *06/*

62

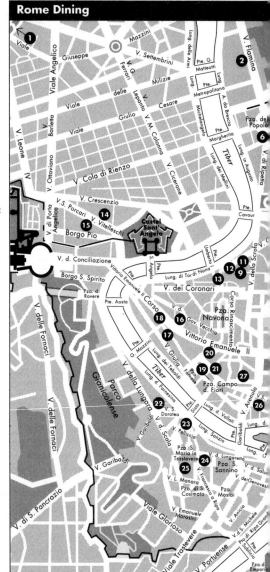

Rome Dining

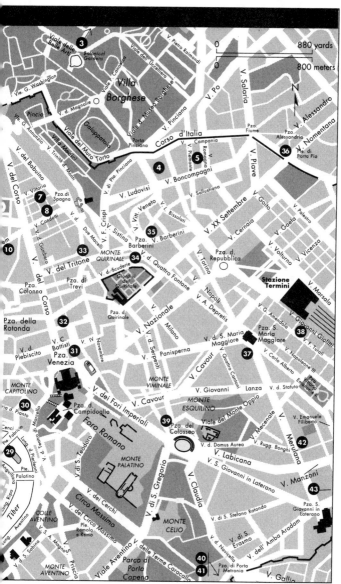

35091. Jacket and tie. AE, DC, MC, V. No lunch. Closed Sun. and Mon.

\$\$\$\$ ✕ **Le Jardin.** Located in the Parioli residential district, this restaurant is famous for its chichi crowd. It's in the exclusive Lord Byron hotel, itself a triumph of studied interior decoration. The imaginative menu is a tempting compendium of seasonal specialties served with newer-than-now nouvelle style. If they are on the menu, try the risotto with seafood and vegetable sauce or the fillet of beef with morels. ✉ *Hotel Lord Byrokn, Via Giuseppe De Notaris 5,* ☎ *06/322–0404. Reservations essential. Jacket and tie. AE, DC, MC, V. Closed Sun. and Aug.*

\$\$\$\$ ✕ **Les Etoiles.** If you're looking for an ascension-into-heaven
★ moment when dining in Rome, just book a window table at this restaurant. As candles flicker at your side, enjoy the *nuova cucina* (the Italian variation of nouvelle cuisine) specials and sit back and watch the blue fade out of the dome of St. Peter's. The rooftop restaurant of the Atlante Star hotel, in the Prati section of Rome, has big window walls to frame the breathtaking view of the Vatican, which is especially magical later in the evening when the cupola's graceful curves are illuminated. The menu varies, depending on what the chef chooses at the market. There are interesting pasta dishes with porcini mushrooms or seasonal vegetables, classic or creative risotto (for two), fresh seafood, and choice grilled meats. When you reserve, ask for a table with a view of St. Peter's. ✉ *Hotel Atlante Star, Via dei Bastioni 1,* ☎ *06/689–3434. Reservations essential. Jacket and tie. AE, DC, MC, V.*

\$\$\$\$ ✕ **Sans Souci.** All the glitz and glamour of the dolce vita days of Rome in the 1950s lives on in this overdecorated but superb downstairs sanctuary of gourmet delights. Service is literally fit for a king—and the Sans Souci has had a few among its customers, along with Hollywood biggies and business magnates. It is the only restaurant in Rome with a doorman, but don't let that intimidate you, for the staff is courteous and attentive. The menu presents both French and Italian dishes, among them truffled terrine de foie gras and *agnello al timo* (roast lamb with thyme). ✉ *Via Sicilia 20,* ☎ *06/482–1814. Reservations essential. Jacket and tie. AE, DC, MC, V. No lunch. Closed Mon. and mid-Aug.–Sept. 6.*

$$$ ✕ **Coriolano.** The only tourists who find their way to this classic restaurant near Porta Pia are likely to be gourmets looking for quintessential Italian food, and that means light homemade pastas, choice olive oil, and market-fresh ingredients, especially seafood. The small dining room is decorated with antiques, and tables are set with immaculate white linen, sparkling crystal, and silver. Although seafood dishes vary, *tagliolini all'aragosta* (thin noodles with lobster sauce) is usually on the menu, as are porcini mushrooms in season (cooked according to a secret recipe). The wine list is predominantly Italian, but includes some French and California wines, too. ✉ *Via Ancona 14,* ☎ *06/442–49863. Jacket and tie. AE, DC, MC, V. Closed Sun.; Sat. in July; and Aug. 1–25.*

$$$ ✕ **Corsetti—Il Galeone.** Located on a market square in Trastevere, this spot is decorated like an old galleon, lined with well-seasoned wood and laded with nautical accessories. Seafood is the specialty, but you will also find an ample selection of typical Roman pastas and meat dishes, as well as the famous carciofi alla romana. ✉ *Piazza San Cosimato 27,* ☎ *06/581–6311. AE, DC, MC, V. Closed Wed.*

$$$ ✕ **Da Checcho er Carrettiere.** You'll find Da Checcho tucked away behind Piazza Trilussa in Trastevere. It has the look of a country inn, with hanging braids of garlic and an antipasto table that features some unusual specialties, such as a well-seasoned mashed potato-and-tomato mixture. Among the hearty pasta offerings are spaghetti *alla carrettiera* (with black pepper, sharp cheese, and olive oil), and linguine with scampi. Seafood (which can be expensive) is the main feature on the menu, but traditional Roman meat dishes are offered, too. This is a great place to soak up genuine Trastevere color and hospitality. ✉ *Via Benedetta 10,* ☎ *06/581–7018. Reservations essential. AE, DC, MC, V. No dinner Sun. Closed Mon. and Aug. 10–Sept. 10.*

$$$ ✕ **Il Convivio.** Don't be intimidated by the opaque glass, closed door, and doorbell at the entrance. This, as its name suggests, is a convivial little restaurant, and it is earning a reputation as one of Rome's best. Reservations are essential, for it accommodates only 30 diners. The food is what it's all about: classic Italian (and Roman) dishes prepared with flair and a brilliant use of herbs, as in shellfish with tarragon and lamb with thyme. The *menù degustazione* (tasting menu) is good value. ⊠ *Via dell'Orso 44,* ☎ *06/686–9432. Reservations essential. AE, DC, MC, V. Closed Sun.*

$$$ ✕ **Passetto.** Benefiting from a choice location near Piazza Navona, Passetto has been a favorite with Italians and tourists for many years: It's a place you can rely on for classic Italian food and courteous service. If you can, eat on the terrace—it's especially memorable at night; the mirrored dining room is more staid. Roman specialties, such as cannelloni and abbacchio, are featured. ⊠ *Via Zanardelli 14,* ☎ *06/654–0569. Jacket and tie. AE, DC, MC, V. No lunch Mon. Closed Sun.*

$$$ ✕ **Piperno.** A favorite, in the old Jewish ghetto next to historic Palazzo Cenci, Piperno has been in business for more than a century. It is *the* place to go for Rome's extraordinary carciofi alla giudia. You eat in three small wood-paneled dining rooms or at one of a handful of tables outdoors. Try *filetti di* baccalà (fillet of cod), pasta *e ceci* (a thick soup of pasta tubes and chickpeas), *fiori di zucca* (stuffed zucchini flowers), and artichokes. ⊠ *Monte dei Cenci 9,* ☎ *06/654–2772. AE, DC, MC, V. No dinner Sun. Closed Mon., Dec. 25, Easter, and Aug.*

$$$ ✕ **Ranieri.** Walk down a quiet street off fashionable Via Con-
★ dotti, near the Spanish Steps, to find this historic restaurant, founded by a one-time chef of Queen Victoria. Ranieri remains a favorite for its traditional atmosphere and decor, with damask-covered walls, velvet banquettes, crystal chandeliers, and old paintings. The Italian-French cuisine is excellent: Portions are abundant, and checks remain comfortably in the low end of this price category. Among the many specialties on the vast menu are *gnocchetti alla parigina* (feather-light dumplings with cheese sauce) and *mignonettes alla Regina Vittoria* (veal with pâté and an eight-cheese sauce). ⊠ *Via Mario dei Fiori 26,* ☎ *06/678–6505. Reservations essential. AE, DC, MC, V. Closed Sun.*

$$$ ✕ **Vecchia Roma.** It's everything a Roman restaurant should
★ be. Two decades ago, discerning American travelers realized that Vecchia Roma was too special to be left to the Romans—so they've made it their own. Exceptional cuisine, beautiful setting, gracious service—it all adds up to a deliciously sublime evening. Tucked away on a frozen-in-time piazza near the Campidoglio, Vecchia Roma has an airy and polished interior of beige walls and frescoed ac-

cents. It is a decor that is quintessentially Roman—a testament to rich simplicity and unpretentious nobility. The same can be said of the food. Together with classic Roman specialties, it features a range of main-course salads in summer and a wide choice of sauces served with polenta in the winter. Romans in the know always choose the seasonal specialties—such as porcini, mushrooms that taste just like filet mignon—which can be extraordinary. During fine weather, dining at one of the tables set up on the piazza will lend a very special flavor to your meal. As Vecchia Roma's fame has spread, it has maintained its high standards: Let's hope this will continue to be the case. ⊠ *Piazza Campitelli 18,* ☎ *06/686–4604. Reservations essential. AE, DC. Closed Wed. and mid-Aug.*

\$\$ ✕ **Cannavota.** On the square next to San Giovanni in Laterano, Cannavota has a large and faithful following and has fed generations of neighborhood families over the years. Seafood dominates, but carnivores are catered to, also. Try one of the pastas with seafood sauce—fettuccine with shrimp scampi is a good choice—and then go on to grilled fish or meat. The cheerful atmosphere and rustic decor make for an authentically Roman experience. ⊠ *Piazza San Giovanni in Laterano 20,* ☎ *06/772–05007. AE, DC, MC, V. Closed Wed. and Aug. 1–20.*

\$\$ ✕ **Colline Emiliane.** Not far from Piazza Barberini this unassuming trattoria offers exceptionally good food. Behind an opaque glass facade are a couple of plain dining rooms, where you are served light homemade pastas, a special chicken broth, and meats ranging from boiled beef to *giambonetto di vitella* (roast veal) and *cotoletta alla bolognese* (veal cutlet with cheese and tomato sauce). Family-run, it's quiet and soothing—a good place to rest after a sightseeing stint. Service is cordial and discreet. ⊠ *Via degli Avignonesi 22,* ☎ *06/481–7538. No credit cards. Closed Fri. and Aug.*

\$\$ ✕ **Costanza.** In Rome, one man's archaeological site can be another man's eatery. As its ancient Roman brickwork reveals, this fashionable trattoria occupies a small part of the Theater of Pompey, where Julius Caesar met his end. Serious gourmands rave about this spot, which has become a meeting place for artists, actors, and politicos. The mixed hot and cold antipasto is a specialty, as are crêpes with mushrooms and risotto with zucchini flowers. ⊠ *Piazza del Paradiso 65,* ☏ *06/ 686–1717. AE, DC, MC, V. Closed Sun. and Aug.*

$$ ✕ **Dal Bolognese.** Long a favorite with the art crowd, this classic restaurant on Piazza del Popolo is a trendy choice for a leisurely lunch between sightseeing and shopping. While dining, feast your eyes on an extensive array of contemporary paintings and check out the clientele, many of whom are wearing the latest Fendi turnout. As the name of the restaurant promises, the cooking here adheres to the hearty tradition of Bologna, with homemade pastas in creamy sauces and steaming trays of boiled meats. For dessert, there's *dolce della mamma* (a concoction of ice cream, zabaglione, and chocolate sauce). ⊠ *Piazza del Popolo 1,* ☏ *06/361–1426. DC, V. Closed Mon. and Aug. 7–22.*

$$ ✕ **La Campana.** This inconspicuous trattoria off Via della Scrofa has a venerable history: There has been an inn on this spot since the 15th century, and the two plain dining rooms occupy what were once stables. It's a homey place, with friendly waiters, snowy white linens on close-set tables, and good Roman food at reasonable prices. The menu offers specialties like *vignarola* (sautéed fava beans, peas, and artichokes), rigatoni with prosciutto and tomato sauce, and *olivette di vitello con purée* (tiny veal rolls with mashed potatoes). ⊠ *Vicolo della Campana 18,* ☏ *06/686–7820. AE, DC, MC, V. Closed Mon. and Aug.*

$$ ✕ **Le Maschere.** For a taste of southern Italian (Calabrian) fare, look for this cellar restaurant hidden away between Largo Argentina and Piazza Campo dei Fiori. A couple of planters, with a few outdoor tables in summer, mark this informal spot. Downstairs you pass an impressive antipasto buffet, and a pizza oven glows in a corner of the dining room. Dark rustic walls are hung with everything from paper garlands to old utensils; there are pottery wine jugs and rush-bottom chairs. Order spicy Calabria salami to start and then go on to pizza or southern favorites such as pasta with broccoli or with tomato and eggplant sauce. Grilled meat and seafood make up the list of second courses. Music on weekends and efficient service make for a pleasant evening. ⊠ *Via Monte della Farina 29,* ☏ *06/687–9444. AE, DC, MC, V. No lunch. Closed Mon. and mid-Aug.–mid-Sept.*

$$ ✕ **Mariano.** Near Via Veneto, Mariano (who is actually Tonino, Mariano's son-in-law and successor) is an exponent of quality and tradition. Since he leaves flights of culinary fancy to others, you can be sure of finding authentic Roman and central-Italian cuisine here, including delicate egg pastas, game, and abbacchio in season. ⊠ *Via Piemonte 79,* ☎ *06/474–5256. AE, DE, MC, V. No lunch Sat. Closed Sun.*

$$ ✕ **Orso 80.** This bright and bustling trattoria is in Old Rome, on a street famed for artisans' workshops. It has both a Roman and an international following, and is known, above all, for a fabulous antipasto table. Try the homemade egg pasta or the bucatini all'amatriciana; there's plenty of seafood on the menu, too. For dessert, the ricotta cake, a genuine Roman specialty, is always good. ⊠ *Via dell'Orso 33,* ☎ *06/686–4904. AE, DC, MC, V. Closed Mon. and Aug. 10–20.*

$$ ✕ **Osteria da Nerone.** Between the Colosseum and the church of San Pietro in Vincoli, this family-run trattoria features a tempting antipasto table and fresh pastas. The specialty is fettuccine *al Nerone* (with peas, salami, and mushrooms), but the homemade ravioli are good, too. In fair weather you eat outdoors with a view of the Colosseum. ⊠ *Via Terme di Tito 96,* ☎ *06/474–5207. Closed Sun. and mid-Aug.*

$$ ✕ **Otello alla Concordia.** The clientele in this popular spot—it's off a shopping street near Piazza di Spagna—is about evenly divided between tourists and workers from shops and offices in the area. The former like to sit outdoors in the courtyard in any weather; the latter have their regular tables in one of the inside dining rooms. The menu offers classic Roman and Italian dishes, and service is friendly and efficient. Since every tourist in Rome knows about it, and since the regulars won't relinquish their niches, you may have to wait for a table; go early. ⊠ *Via della Croce 81,* ☎ *06/678–1454. Reservations not accepted. AE, DC. Closed Sun. and Dec. 25.*

$$ ✕ **Paris.** On a small square just off Piazza Santa Maria in Trastevere, Paris (named after a former owner, not the city) has a reassuring, understated ambience, without the hokey, folky flamboyance of so many eating places in this gentrified neighborhood. It also has a menu featuring the best of classic Roman cuisine: homemade fettuccine, delicate fritto misto and, of course, baccalà. In fair weather opt for tables on the little piazza. ⊠ *Piazza San Callisto 7/a,* ☏ *06/ 581–5378. AE, DC, MC, V. No dinner Sun. Closed Mon. and 3 wks in Aug.*

$$ ✕ **Pierluigi.** Pierluigi, in the heart of Old Rome, is a long-time favorite with foreign residents of Rome and Italians in the entertainment field. On busy evenings it's almost impossible to find a table, so make sure you reserve well in advance. Seafood dominates (if you're in the mood to splurge, try the lobster), but traditional Roman dishes are offered, too, including *orecchiette* (ear-shape pasta) con broccoli and simple spaghetti. Eat in the pretty piazza in summer. ⊠ *Piazza dei Ricci 144,* ☏ *06/686–8717. AE, V. Closed Mon. and 2 wks in Aug.*

$$ ✕ **Romolo.** Nowhere else do the lingering rays of the set-
★ ting Roman sun seem more inviting than from the tavern garden of this charming Trastevere haunt—reputedly the one-time home of Raphael's lady love, the Fornarina. Generations of Romans and tourists have enjoyed its romantic courtyard and historic dining room, where, in the evening, strolling musicians serenade diners. The cuisine is appropriately Roman; specialties include mozzarella *alla fornarina* (deep-fried, with ham and anchovies) and *braciolette d'abbacchio scottadito* (grilled baby lamb chops). Alternatively, try one of the new vegetarian pastas featuring carciofi or radicchio. Meats are charcoal-grilled; there's also a wood-burning oven. ⊠ *Via di Porta Settimiana 8,* ☏ *06/ 581–8284. AE, DC, V. Closed Mon. and Aug. 2–23.*

$$ ✕ **Sora Lella.** What was once a simple trattoria ensconced on the Tiberina Island is now a monument to the late foundress herself, beloved example of true Roman warmth and personality. And although prices are much higher than when Sora Lella presided over the cash desk, the cooking is still 100% Roman. Rigatoni all'amatriciana and *seppie con piselli* (cuttlefish stewed with tomatoes and peas) are usually on the menu, but leave room for the quintessential Roman ricotta cake. ⊠ *Via Ponte Quattro Capi 16,* ☏ *06/ 686–1601. AE, MC, V. Closed Sun. and Aug.*

$$ ✕ **Tana del Grillo.** Near Santa Maria Maggiore, this family-run restaurant features the specialties of one of Italy's least-known regional cuisines—that of Ferrara. Sausages and salami of various types, gnocchi and lasagna or *pasticcio* *di maccheroni* (pasta casserole) are typical dishes, but the pièce de résistance is the *bollito*, a steaming cart laded with several types of boiled meat, which the waiter will carve to your order. ⊠ *Via Alfieri 4,* ☎ *06/704–53517. AE, DC, MC, V. No lunch Mon. Closed Sun.*

$$ ✕ **Tullio.** This Tuscan trattoria off Via Veneto and Piazza Barberini opened in the dolce vita days of the 1950s, when this area was the center of Roman chic and bohemian life. It soon acquired a faithful clientele of politicians, journalists, and artists, and it has changed little over the years. Decor and menu are simple. The latter offers typically Tuscan pasta *e fagioli* (with beans), grilled steaks and chops, and fagioli *all'uccelletto* (with tomato and sage). ⊠ *Via San Nicolò da Tolentino 26,* ☎ *06/481–8564. Reservations essential. AE, DC, MC, V. Closed Sun. and Aug.*

$ ✕ **Abruzzi.** Here's a simple trattoria off Piazza Santi Apostoli near Piazza Venezia that specializes in the regional cooking of the mountainous Abruzzo region, southeast of Rome. *Tonnarelli* (square pasta) is served with mushrooms, peas, and ham or with a meat sauce. Baby lamb is another classic regional dish. ⊠ *Via del Vaccaro 1,* ☎ *06/679–3897. V. Closed Sat. and Aug.*

$ ✕ **Baffetto.** The emphasis here is on good old-fashioned value: Baffetto is Rome's best-known inexpensive pizza restaurant, plainly decorated and very popular. You'll probably have to wait in line outside on the cobblestones and then share your table once inside. The interior is mostly given over to the ovens, the tiny cash desk, and the simple, paper-covered tables. *Bruschetta* (toast) and *crostini* (mozzarella toast) are the only variations on the pizza theme. Turnover is fast: This is not the place to linger over your meal. ⊠ *Via del Governo Vecchio 114,* ☎ *06/686–1617. Reservations not accepted. No credit cards. No lunch. Closed Sun. and Aug.*

$ ✕ **Birreria Tempera.** This old-fashioned beer hall is very busy ★ at lunchtime, when it's invaded by businesspeople and students from the Piazza Venezia area. There's a good selection of salads and cold cuts, as well as pasta and daily specials. Bavarian-style specialties such as goulash and wurst and sauerkraut prevail in the evening, when light and dark Italian beers flow freely. ⊠ *Via San Marcello 19,* ☎ *06/678–6203. Reservations not accepted. No credit cards. Closed Sun. and Aug.*

$ ✗ **Cottini.** For lunch or supper, this cafeteria on the corner of Piazza Santa Maria Maggiore is reliable; the food counter and tables are in the back, beyond the large coffee bar and pastry counters. Salads, hot pastas, and main courses are always fresh, and they are served with a smile. The in-house bakery provides such tempting desserts as crème caramel and chocolate cake. ⊠ *Via Merulana 287,* ☎ *06/474–0768. Reservations not accepted. No credit cards. Closed Mon.*

$ ✗ **Fagianetto.** Massive wooden beams on high are as solid as the reputation of this family-run trattoria near Termini Station. It has a regular neighborhood clientele, but also satisfies tourists' appetites with a special menu for about 20,000 lire. But you may well be tempted by à la carte offerings such as rigatoni *alla norcina* (with a sauce of crumbled sausage and cream) or osso buco *con funghi* (with mushrooms). Service is swift and courteous. ⊠ *Via Filippo Turati 21,* ☎ *06/446–7306. AE, DC, MC, V. Closed Mon.*

$ ✗ **Fratelli Menghi.** Neighborhood regulars frequent this trattoria that has been in the same family for as long as anyone can remember (a portrait of Pop is on the wall in one dining room) and produces typical Roman fare. There's usually a thick hearty soup such as minestrone, and other standbys, including *involtini* (meat roulades). ⊠ *Via Flaminia 57,* ☎ *06/320–0803. Reservations not accepted. No credit cards. Closed Sun.*

$ ✗ **Grappolo d'Oro.** This centrally located trattoria off
★ Campo dei Fiori has been a favorite for decades with locals and foreign residents, one of whom wrote it up in the *New Yorker* some years ago. This measure of notoriety has not induced the graying, courteous owners to change their two half-paneled dining rooms or menu, which features pasta all'amatriciana and scaloppine any way you want them. Inquire about the day's special. ⊠ *Piazza della Cancelleria 80,* ☎ *06/686–4118. AE, MC, V. Closed Sun.*

$ ✗ **Perilli.** A bastion of authentic Roman cooking and trattoria atmosphere since 1913, this is the place to go to try rigatoni *con pagliata* (with baby lamb's intestines)—if you're into that sort of thing. Otherwise the all'amatriciana and carbonara sauces are classics. The house wine is a golden nectar from the Castelli Romani. ⊠ *Via Marmorata 39,* ☎ *06/574–2415. No credit cards. Closed Wed.*

$ ✕ **Polese.** It's best to come here in good weather, when you can sit outdoors under trees and look out on the charming square off Corso Vittorio Emanuele in Old Rome. Like most centrally located inexpensive eateries in Rome, it is crowded on weekends and weekday evenings in the summer. Straightforward Roman specialties include fettuccine *alla Polese* (with cream and mushrooms) and *vitello alla fornara* (roast brisket of veal with potatoes). ✉ *Piazza Sforza Cesarini 40,* ☎ *06/686–1709. AE, DC, MC, V. Closed Tues., 15 days in Aug., and 15 days in Dec.*

$ ✕ **Pollarola.** This typical Roman trattoria, near Piazza Navona and Campo dei Fiori, has artificial flowers on the tables but—as a special feature—it also has an ancient, authentic Roman column embedded in the rear wall. You can eat outdoors in fair weather. Try a pasta specialty such as fettuccine with creamy gorgonzola sauce and a mixed plate from the array of fresh antipasti. The house wines, white or red, are good. ✉ *Piazza della Pollarola 24 (Campo dei Fiori),* ☎ *06/6880–1654. AE, V. Closed Sun.*

$ ✕ **Tavernetta.** The central location—between the Trevi Fountain and the Spanish Steps—and the good-value tourist menu make this a reliable bet for a simple but filling meal. The menu features Sicilian and Abruzzese specialties; try the pasta with eggplant or the *porchetta* (roast suckling pig). Both the red and the white house wines are good. ✉ *Via del Nazareno 3,* ☎ *06/679–3124. Reservations essential. AE, DC, MC, V. Closed Mon. and Aug.*

$ ✕ **Tre Pupazzi.** The "three puppets" after which the trattoria is named are the worn stone figures on a fragment of an ancient sarcophagus that embellishes a building on this byway near the Vatican. The tavern, founded in 1625, wears its centuries lightly, upholding a tradition of good food, courteous service, and reasonable prices. The menu offers classic Roman/Abruzzese trattoria fare, including fettuccine and abbacchio, plus pizzas at lunchtime (a rarity in Rome) and well past midnight. ✉ *Via dei Tre Pupazzi at Borgo Pio,* ☎ *06/686–8371. AE, MC, V. Closed Sun.*

Along Via Appia Antica

$$ ✕ **Cecilia Metella.** From the entrance on Via Appia Antica, practically opposite the catacombs, you walk uphill to a low-lying but sprawling construction designed for wedding feasts and banquets. There's a large terrace shaded by vines for outdoor dining. Although obviously geared to larger groups, Cecilia Metella also gives couples and small groups full attention, good service, and fine Roman-style cuisine. The specialties are the searing-hot *crespelle* (crêpes), served in individual casseroles, and *pollo al Nerone* (chicken à la Nero; flambéed, of course). ⊠ *Via Appia Antica 125,* ☎ *06/513–6743. AE, MC, V. Closed Mon. and last 2 wks in Aug.*

$$ ✕ **L'Archeologia.** In this farmhouse just beyond the catacombs, you dine indoors beside the fireplace in cool weather or in the garden under age-old vines in the summer. The atmosphere is friendly and intimate, and specialties include homemade pastas, abbacchio scottadito, seafood, and some Greek dishes. ⊠ *Via Appia Antica 139,* ☎ *06/788–0494. AE, MC, V. Closed Thurs.*

4 Lodging

THE WIDE RANGE of Roman accommodations are graded according to regional standards, from five stars down to one. Palatial surroundings, luxurious comfort, and high standards of service can be taken for granted in the city's five-star ($$$$) establishments, but in other categories, especially $$ and $, standards vary considerably. Fortunately for tourists, many Rome hotels have upgraded their facilities, readjusting their rates only slightly. In general, Fodor's hotel choices for Rome have been made with an eye to good value and convenient location. The old-fashioned Roman pensione no longer exists as an official category, but, although now graded as inexpensive hotels, some preserve the homey atmosphere that makes visitors prefer them, especially for longer stays.

There are distinct advantages to staying in a hotel within easy walking distance of the main sights, particularly now that so much of downtown Rome is closed to daytime traffic. You can leave your car at a garage and explore by foot. One disadvantage, however, is noise, because the Romans are a voluble people—with or without cars to add to the racket. Ask for an inside room if you are a light sleeper, but don't be disappointed if it faces a dark courtyard.

Because Rome's religious importance makes it a year-round tourist destination, there is never a period when hotels are predictably empty, so you should always try to make reservations, even if only a few days in advance, by phone or fax. Always inquire about special low rates, often available in both winter and summer if occupancy is low.

Room rates in Rome are on a par with, or even higher than, those in most other European capitals, but a favorable exchange rate can make them more attractive. Ask whether the room rate includes breakfast. An extra charge, anything from 7,000 to 27,000 lire depending on the category of hotel, may be added for this, but remember that you're not obliged to take breakfast in the hotel. If you don't want to, make this clear when you check in. Air-conditioning in lower-priced hotels may cost extra; in more expensive hotels it will be included in the price. All hotels have rate cards on the room doors or inside the closet. These specify exactly what you have to pay and detail any extras. If business is slack, hotels in all categories may give you a discount rate. Ask for *la tariffa scontata* (the discount rate).

CATEGORY	COST*
$$$$	over 450,000 lire
$$$	300,000–450,000 lire
$$	220,000–300,000 lire
$	under 220,000 lire

All prices are for a standard double room for two, including tax and service.

$$$$ 🏨 **Cavalieri Hilton.** Though the Cavalieri is outside the imaginary confines of the city's center, distance has its advantages, one of them being the magnificent view from the hotel's hilltop site (ask for a room facing the city). This hotel is an oasis of quiet and comfort. Good taste and a distinctive Italian flair keynoted extensive renovations and redecorating in 1994. If you can tear yourself away from your balcony, the terraces, gardens, and swimming pool, you will find a courtesy shuttle bus leaving for Piazza Barberini in the center of Rome every 30 minutes. ⊠ *Via Cadlolo 101,* ☎ *06/35091,* 🖷 *06/3509–2241. 376 rooms and suites with bath. 2 restaurants, bar, pool, health club. AE, DC, MC, V.*

$$$$ 🏨 **Eden.** A hotel for whispered superlatives in praise of its dashing elegance and stunning vistas of Rome, the Eden was once the preferred haunt of Hemingway, Ingrid Bergman, and Fellini, and of many celebrities before them. It was totally renovated and reopened in 1994 under the aegis of the Forte group. Precious antiques, sumptuous Italian fabrics, linen sheets, and marble baths create an atmosphere of understated elegance. The views from the rooftop bar and restaurant will take your breath away, and the cuisine merits raves, too. ⊠ *Via Ludovisi 49,* ☎ *06/474–3551,* 🖷 *06/482–1584. 112 rooms and suites with bath. Restaurant, bar, exercise room, parking. AE, DC, MC, V.*

$$$$ 🏨 **Excelsior.** To Romans and many others, the white Victorian cupola of the Excelsior is a symbol of Rome at its most cosmopolitan. The hotel's porte cochere has sheltered Europe's aristocrats and Hollywood's royalty as they alighted from their Rollses and Ferraris. They entered the polished doors that still open onto a world of luxury lav-

78

Rome Lodging

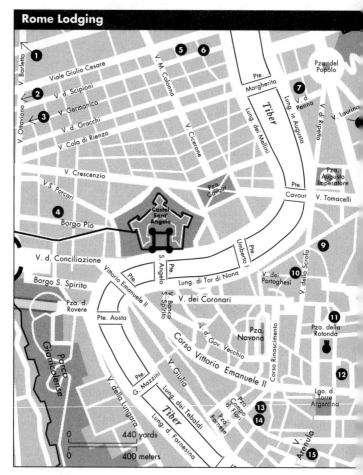

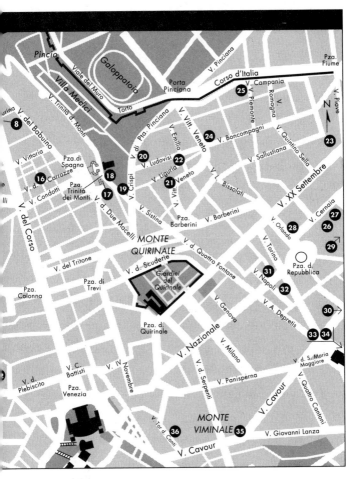

ished with mirrors, carved moldings, Oriental rugs, crystal chandeliers, and huge, baroque floral arrangements. The theme of gracious living prevails throughout the hotel in splendidly appointed rooms and marble baths. ⊠ *Via Veneto 125,* ☎ *06/4708,* FAX *06/482–6205. 377 rooms and suites with bath. Restaurant, bar, barbershop, beauty salon, parking. AE, DC, MC, V.*

$$$$ ⊞ **Grand.** A 100-year-old establishment of class and style, this hotel caters to an elite international clientele. It's only a few minutes from Via Veneto. Off the richly decorated, split-level main salon—where afternoon tea is served every day—there are a smaller, intimate bar and a buffet restaurant. The spacious bedrooms are decorated in gracious empire style, with smooth fabrics and thick carpets in tones of blue and pale gold. Crystal chandeliers and marble baths add a luxurious note. The Grand also offers one of Italy's most beautiful dining rooms, called simply Le Restaurant. ⊠ *Via Vittorio Emanuele Orlando 3,* ☎ *06/4709,* FAX *06/ 474–7307. 170 rooms and suites with bath. 2 restaurants, bar, beauty salon, sauna, parking. AE, DC, MC, V.*

$$$$ ⊞ **Hassler.** Located at the top of the Spanish Steps, the
★   Hassler boasts sweeping views of Rome from its front rooms and penthouse restaurant; other rooms overlook the gardens of Villa Medici. The hotel is run by the distinguished Wirth family of hoteliers, which assures a cordial atmosphere and magnificent service from the well-trained staff. The public rooms have an extravagant 1950s elegance—especially the first-floor bar, a chic rendezvous, and the glass-roofed lounge, with gold marble walls and a hand-painted tile floor. The comfortable guest rooms are decorated in a variety of classic styles, some with frescoed walls. The penthouse suite has a mirrored ceiling in the bedroom and a huge terrace. ⊠ *Piazza Trinità dei Monti 6,* ☎ *06/678–2651,* FAX *06/678–9991. 101 rooms and suites with bath. Restaurant, bar. AE, DC, MC, V.*

$$$$ ⊞ **Majestic.** In the 19th-century tradition of grand hotels, this establishment on Via Veneto offers sumptuous furnishings and spacious rooms, with up-to-date accessories such as CNN-TV, minibars, strongboxes, and white marble bathrooms. There are authentic antiques in the public rooms, and the excellent restaurant looks like a Victorian conservatory. The Ninfa grill/café on street level is an intimate venue for light meals and drinks. ⊠ *Via Veneto 50,* ☎ *06/486841,* FAX *06/488-0984. 95 rooms and suites with bath, many with whirlpool baths. Restaurant, bar, parking. AE, DC, MC, V.*

$$$$ ⊞ **Minerva.** The Holiday Inn Crowne Plaza Minerva is the very stylish reincarnation of the hostelry that occupied this 17th-century palazzo for centuries, hosting literati from Stendhal to Sartre and de Beauvoir. Entirely redone, with a stunning new stained-glass lobby ceiling designed by renowned architect Paolo Portoghesi, the Minerva has everything a guest could want in the way of comfort, all in an absolutely central location. And from the roof terrace you can almost touch the immense, flattened dome of Hadrian's Pantheon. ⊠ *Piazza della Minerva 69,* ☎ *06/ 6994-1888,* FAX *06/679-4165. 134 rooms with bath. Restaurant, bar. AE, DC, MC, V.*

$$$ ⊞ **Albergo del Sole al Pantheon.** This small hotel has been in its central location opposite the Pantheon since the 15th century. It was entirely renovated in 1989 and has been tastefully decorated with a blend of modern and antique furnishings. Ceilings are high, floors are tiled in terra-cotta, and there is a charming courtyard for alfresco breakfast in good weather. ⊠ *Piazza della Rotonda 63,* ☎ *06/678-0441,* FAX *06/684-0689. 26 rooms with bath. Bar. AE, DC, MC, V.*

$$$ ⊞ **Farnese.** A turn-of-the-century mansion, totally renovated
★ in 1991, the Farnese is near the Metro and within walking distance of St. Peter's. Furnished with great attention to detail in Art Deco style, it has dazzling modern baths and charming fresco decorations. Room rates are low for the category and include a banquet-size breakfast. ⊠ *Via Alessandro Farnese 30,* ☎ *06/321-2553,* FAX *06/321- 5129. 24 rooms with bath. Bar, parking, roof garden. AE, DC, MC, V.*

$$$
★   🏨 **Forum.** A centuries-old palace converted into a fine
hotel, the Forum is on a quiet street within shouting dis-
tance of the Roman Forum and Piazza Venezia. Although
it seems tucked away out of the mainstream, it's actually
handy to all the main sights. The wood-paneled lobby and
street-level bar are warm and welcoming. The smallish
bedrooms are furnished in rich pink and beige fabrics; the
bathrooms are ample, with either tub or shower. What's
really special, though, is the rooftop restaurant and bar: The
view toward the Colosseum is superb. Breakfast or a night-
cap up here can be memorable. ⊠ *Via Tor dei Conti 25,*
☎ *06/679–2446,* 🖷 *06/678–6479. 76 rooms with bath.*
Restaurant, bar. AE, DC, MC, V.

$$$ 🏨 **Giulio Cesare.** An aristocratic town house in the resi-
dential, but central, Prati district, the Giulio Cesare is a 10-
minute walk across the Tiber from Piazza del Popolo. It's
beautifully run, with a friendly staff and a quietly luxurious air. The rooms are elegantly furnished, with chandeliers, thick rugs, floor-length drapes, and rich damasks in
soft colors. Public rooms have Oriental carpets, old prints
and paintings, marble fireplaces, and a grand piano. ⊠ *Via
degli Scipioni 287,* ☎ *06/321–0751,* 🖷 *06/321–1736. 90
rooms with bath. Bar, garden. AE, DC, MC, V.*

$$$ 🏨 **Victoria.** A 1950s luxury in the public rooms, solid com-
fort throughout, and impeccable management are the main
features of this hotel near Via Veneto. Oriental rugs, oil paint-
ings, welcoming armchairs, and fresh flowers add charm
to the public spaces, and the rooms are well furnished with
armchairs and other amenities ignored by many modern dec-
orators. American businessmen, who prize the hotel's per-
sonalized service and restful atmosphere, are frequent
guests. Some upper rooms and the roof terrace overlook
the majestic pines of Villa Borghese. ⊠ *Via Campania 41,*
☎ *06/473931,* 🖷 *06/487–1890. 110 rooms with bath.*
Restaurant, bar. AE, DC, MC, V.

$$ 🏨 **Art Deco.** This hotel's name tells all about its glamorous
decor, attuned to the elegance and fancy of the 1920s, with
whimsical accents in Deco paintings and antiques. Under-
lying the style is reassuring technology: a fail-safe electrical system, key cards, air-conditioning, and whirlpool baths.

You can breakfast on the roof terrace. The hotel is in a residential neighborhood 10 minutes from Termini Station and handy to public transport. Book through Best Western for the best rates. ⊠ *Via Palestro 19,* ☎ *06/445–7588,* FAX *06/ 444–1483. 49 rooms with bath. Restaurant, bar. AE, DC, MC, V.*

$$ ⛩ **Britannia.** This fine small hotel is a very special place, offering superior quality at moderate rates. Its quiet but central location is one attraction; a caring management is another. Guests are coddled with English-language dailies and local weather reports delivered to their rooms each morning, and with sybaritic marble bathrooms and well-furnished rooms. Even if you don't choose one of the top-floor terrace rooms, you can still enjoy the splendid Roman panorama, actually a marvelous wraparaound painting, which lights up the breakfast room and its ample buffet. ⊠ *Via Napoli 64,* ☎ *06/488–3153,* FAX *06/488–2343. 32 rooms with bath. 2 bars. AE, DC, MC, V.*

$$ ⛩ **Carriage.** The Carriage's location is what makes it special: It's just two blocks away from the Spanish Steps, in the heart of Rome. The stylish decor uses subdued Baroque accents and antique reproductions to give the hotel a touch of elegance. Though some of the rooms are pint-size, and a couple open onto an air shaft, several have little terraces, and all guests can avail of the roof garden. ⊠ *Via delle Carrozze 36,* ☎ *06/679–3312,* FAX *06/678–8279. 27 rooms and suites with bath. AE, DC, MC, V.*

$$ ⛩ **D'Este.** Within hailing distance of Santa Maria Maggiore and close to Termini Station (you can arrange to be picked up there by the hotel car), this is in a solidly renovated and distinguished 19th-century building. The fresh-looking decor evokes turn-of-the-century comfort, with brass bedsteads and lamps and dark wood period furniture. Rooms are quiet, light, and spacious; many can accommodate family groups. The attentive owner-manager likes to have fresh flowers in the halls and sees that everything works. He encourages inquiries about special rates, particularly during the slack summer months. ⊠ *Via Carlo Alberto 4/b,* ☎ *06/446–5607,* FAX *06/446–5601. 37 rooms with bath. Bar. AE, DC, MC, V.*

$$ ⛩ **Duca d'Alba.** In the Suburra, a neighborhood near the Colosseum and the Roman Forum and rich in genuine

Roman atmosphere, this elegant hotel has made a stylish contribution to the area's ongoing gentrification. The tasteful neo-classic decor is in character with ancient Roman motifs, custom-designed furnishings, and marble bathrooms. All rooms are entirely soundproofed; a few have tiny terraces. The four-bed suite with kitchenette is an excellent money-saving option for a family or a group of friends. This well-run establishment offers exceptionally good value: Rates are at the lowest rung in the category. The attentive staff is another plus. ⊠ *Via Leonina 14,* ☎ *06/484471,* FAX *06/488–4840. 24 rooms with bath or shower. AE, DC, MC, V.*

$$ ⊞ **Internazionale.** It has an excellent location near the top of the Spanish Steps. In a totally renovated building on desirable Via Sistina, it has double-glazed windows to ensure peace and quiet. Rooms on the fourth floor have terraces; the fourth-floor suite has a private terrace and a frescoed ceiling. The decor throughout is in soothing pastel tones, with some antique pieces, mirrors, and chandeliers. Guests relax in small, homey lounges downstairs and begin the day in the pretty breakfast room. ⊠ *Via Sistina 79,* ☎ *06/699–41823,* FAX *06/678–4764. 40 rooms with bath. AE, MC, V.*

$$ ⊞ **La Residenza.** In a converted town house near Via Veneto, ★ this hotel offers first-class comfort and atmosphere at reasonable rates. The canopied entrance, spacious well-furnished lounges, and the bar and terrace are of the type you would expect to find in a deluxe lodging. Rooms, decorated in aquamarine and beige with bentwood furniture, have large closets, color TV, fridge-bar, and air-conditioning; bathrooms have heated towel racks. The clientele is mostly American. Rates include a generous American-style buffet breakfast. ⊠ *Via Emilia 22,* ☎ *06/488–0789,* FAX *06/485721. 27 rooms with bath or shower. Bar, parking. MC, V.*

$$ ⊞ **Locarno.** The central location off Piazza del Popolo helps keep the Locarno a favorite among the art crowd, which also goes for its intimate mood, though some of Locarno's fine fin de siècle character has been lost in renovations. An attempt has been made to retain the hotel's original charm, however, while modernizing the rooms with such additions as electronic safes and air-conditioning. The decor features coordinated prints in wallpaper and fabrics, lacquered wrought-iron beds, and some antiques.

⊠ *Via della Penna 22,* ☎ *06/361–0841,* FAX *06/321–5249. 38 rooms with bath. Bar, lobby lounge. AE, V.*

$$ ★ 🏨 **Marcella.** Known to connoisseurs as one of Rome's best midsize hotels, with the feel of a smaller, more intimate establishment, it is 10 minutes from Via Veneto or Termini Station. Here you can do your sightseeing from the roof terrace, taking in the view while you breakfast. Many rooms also have good views, and they are all furnished with flair, showing a tasteful use of color, floral prints, and mirrored walls, echoing the elegant winter-garden decor of the lounges and bar. The spacious and flexible suites are ideal for families. ⊠ *Via Flavia 106,* ☎ *06/474–6451,* FAX *06/481–5832. 75 rooms with bath. Bar, parking. AE, DC, MC, V.*

$$ ★ 🏨 **Morgana.** An elegantly conceived hotel, the Morgana offers excellent value in a convenient location near Termini Station. From a dashingly marbled lobby to the antique accents in fully carpeted halls and soundproofed rooms decorated with fine fabrics, this hotel shows the management's attention to comfort and detail. The atmosphere is cordial and the rates are low in this category. ⊠ *Via Filippo Turati 33,* ☎ *06/446–7230,* FAX *06/446–9142. 70 rooms with bath. Bar, airport shuttle. AE, DC, MC, V.*

$$ 🏨 **Portoghesi.** In the heart of Old Rome, the Portoghesi is a small hotel with considerable atmosphere. From a tiny lobby, an equally tiny elevator takes you to the quiet bedrooms, all decorated with floral prints and reproduction antique furniture. There's a breakfast room but no restaurant. ⊠ *Via dei Portoghesi 1,* ☎ *06/686–4231,* FAX *06/687–6976. 27 rooms with bath or shower. MC, V.*

$$ 🏨 **Sant'Anna.** An example of the gentrification of the picturesque old Borgo neighborhood in the shadow of St. Peter's, this fashionable small hotel has ample, air-conditioned bedrooms in Deco style. The frescoes in the breakfast room and fountain in the courtyard are typically Roman touches. There is no elevator to take you up to the top floors, but it's worth the climb to stay in one of the spacious attic rooms, each with a little terrace. ⊠ *Borgo Pio 134,* ☎ *06/688–01602,* FAX *06/683–08717. 20 rooms with bath. AE, DC, MC, V.*

$$ 🏨 **Scalinata di Spagna.** An old-fashioned pensione loved by generations of romantics, this tiny hotel is booked solid for months—even years—ahead. The location at the top of the Spanish Steps, the inconspicuous little entrance, the quaint mixtures of styles in the old furniture, and the view from the terrace where you breakfast bring home the privilege of having gained a place in a very special and exclusive inn. And that's why rates for some rooms go over the top of this category. ⊠ *Piazza Trinità dei Monti 17,* ☎ *06/679–3006,* FAX *06/684–0598. 15 rooms with bath. MC, V.*

$$ 🏨 **Siviglia.** You are transported back to a more opulent era in this freshly renovated 19th-century mansion in the quieter residential fringe of the Termini Station area. Like the several embassies in the neighborhood, it, too, has bright flags flying at the entrance. Inside, Venetian glass chandeliers and antique reproduction furniture give the lounges considerable character; rooms are simpler, with a light, airy touch. ⊠ *Via Gaeta 12,* ☎ *06/444–1196,* FAX *06/444–1195. 42 rooms with bath. Bar. AE, MC, V.*

$$ 🏨 **Teatro di Pompeo.** Where else can you breakfast under the ancient stone vaults of Pompey's Theater, historic site of Julius Caesar's assassination? At this intimate and refined little hotel in the heart of Old Rome you are part of that history; at night, guests sleep under restored beamed ceilings that date from the days of Michelangelo. The tastefully furnished rooms offer comfort as well as charm. Book well in advance. ⊠ *Largo del Pallaro 8,* ☎ *06/687–2812,* FAX *06/688–15531. 13 rooms with bath. AE, DC, MC, V.*

$ 🏨 **Alimandi.** On a side street only a block from the Vatican Museums, this family-operated hotel offers excellent value in a neighborhood with moderately priced shops and restaurants. A spiffy lobby and ample lounges, a tavern for night owls, terraces, and roof gardens are some of the perks here. Rooms are spacious, airy, and well-furnished; many can accommodate extra beds. The few rooms without bath are real bargains. ⊠ *Via Tunisi 8,* ☎ *06/397–23948,* FAX *06/397–23943. 32 rooms, 26 with bath. Parking (fee). AE, MC, V.*

$ 🏨 **Amalia.** Handy to the Vatican and the Cola di Rienzo shopping district, this small former pensione is owned and operated by the Consoli family—Amalia and her brothers. On several floors of a 19th-century building, it has large rooms with functional furnishings, TV sets, direct-dial telephones, pictures of angels on the walls, and gleaming marble bathrooms (hair dryers included). The Ottaviano stop of Metro A is a block away. ⊠ *Via Germanico 66,* ☎ *06/397–23354,* 𝖥𝖠𝖷 *06/397–23365. 25 rooms, 21 with bath or shower. Bar. AE, MC, V.*

$ 🖬 **Arenula.** In a four-story building on an age-worn byway off central Via Arenula, on the edge of the picturesque Ghetto neighborhood, this hotel is one of Rome's best values for the price. The all-white interior is luminous and cheerful. Rooms have pale wood furnishings and gleaming new bathrooms, as well as double-glazed windows and air-conditioning. Several have space for extra beds. Breakfast is optional, so the room rate is free and clear of extras. But nobody is perfect, and the catch at the Arenula is that the graceful oval staircase of white marble and wrought iron is the only way up. There is no elevator, so if you're short-winded ask for a room on the first (second by American standards) floor. ⊠ *Via Santa Maria dei Calderari 47 (Via Arenula),* ☎ *06/687–9454,* 𝖥𝖠𝖷 *06/689–6188. 50 rooms with bath. MC, V.*

$ 🖬 **Campo dei Fiori.** Frescoes, exposed brickwork, and picturesque effects throughout this little hotel in Old Rome could well be the work of a set designer. There's an aura of fantasy and romanticism in the decoration, with the layout cleverly designed to make the most of limited space (with a few rooms so compact as to be claustrophobic). Other rooms are larger, and all have an unusual decorative feature of some kind to remind you that you are in the heart of Rome. There is no elevator, but the climb to the roof terrace rewards you with a marvelous view and a place to relax in pleasant weather. Rates for the best rooms exceed the parameters of this price category. ⊠ *Via del Biscione 6,* ☎ *06/688–06865,* 𝖥𝖠𝖷 *06/68–6003. 27 rooms, 14 with bath. MC, V.*

$ 🖬 **Marcus.** The location, down the street from the Spanish Steps, is the premier feature of this small, homelike hotel occupying a large apartment on one floor of an 18th-century cardinal's palazzo. Many rooms have graceful antique fireplaces; otherwise they are furnished in a rather dowdy, old-fashioned style, as seen in the main living room, which has comfortable armchairs and a crystal chandelier. Double-glazed windows keep out most of the noise of central Rome. ⊠ *Via Clementina 94,* ☎ *06/683–00320,* 𝖥𝖠𝖷 *06/683–00312. 15 rooms with bath. AE, MC, V.*

$ 🎨 **Margutta.** This small hotel is centrally located on a quiet
★ side street between the Spanish Steps and Piazza del Popolo.
Lobby and halls are unassuming, but rooms are a pleasant
surprise, with a clean and airy look, attractive wrought-iron
bedsteads, and modern baths. Though it's in an old building, there is an elevator. ⊠ *Via Laurina 34,* ☎ *06/322–3674.*
21 rooms with bath or shower. AE, DC, MC, V.

$ 🎨 **Miami.** Its location in a dignified 19th-century building
on Rome's important Via Nazionale puts this hotel in a
strategic spot for sightseeing, shopping, and getting around
in general; it is on main bus lines and near Termini Station
and the Metro. The marble floors, chrome trim, and dark
colors are brightened by the friendly family-style management. Rooms on the courtyard are quieter. High-season rates
are slightly higher than category guidelines. ⊠ *Via Nazionale*
230, ☎ *06/ 481–7180,* 𝔽𝔸𝕏 *06/484562. 22 rooms with*
bath. AE, DC, MC, V.

$ 🎨 **Montreal.** This is a compact hotel on a central avenue
across the square from Santa Maria Maggiore, only three
blocks from Termini Station, with bus and subway lines close
by. On two floors of an older building, it has been totally
renovated and offers fresh-looking rooms. The owner-man-
agers are pleasant and helpful, and the neighborhood has
plenty of reasonably priced eating places, plus one of
Rome's largest outdoor markets. ⊠ *Via Carlo Alberto 4,*
☎ *06/446–5522,* 𝔽𝔸𝕏 *06/445–7797. 16 rooms with bath*
or shower. MC, V.

$ 🎨 **Romae.** In the better part of the Termini Station neigh-
borhood, the Romae has the advantages of a strategic location (within walking distance of many sights, and handy
to bus and subway lines), a very friendly and helpful management, and good-size rooms that are clean and airy. The
vivid pictures of Rome in the small lobby and breakfast
room, the luminous white walls and light wood furniture
in the bedrooms, and the bright little baths all have a fresh
look. Amenities such as satellite TV and a hair dryer in every
room, and breakfast included in the room rate, make this
hotel a very good value. Families benefit from special rates
and services. ⊠ *Via Palestro 49,* ☎ *06/446–3554,* 𝔽𝔸𝕏 *06/*
446–3914. 20 rooms with bath. AE, MC, V.

5 Nightlife and the Arts

THE ARTS

Rome offers a vast selection of music, dance, opera, and film. Schedules of events are published in daily newspapers; in *Trovaroma,* the weekly entertainment guide published every Thursday as a supplement to the daily *La Repubblica*; in the *Guest in Rome* booklet distributed free at hotel desks; and in flyers available at EPT and city tourist information offices. An English-language periodical, *Wanted in Rome* (1,000 lire), is available at centrally located newsstands and has good listings of events. There are listings in English in the back of the weekly *Romac'è* booklet, with handy bus information for each listing.

Concerts

Rome has long hosted a wide variety of classical music concerts, although it is a common complaint that the city does not have adequate concert halls; a new concert hall is currently under construction. Depending on the location, concert tickets can cost from 15,000 to 50,000 lire. The principal concert series are those of the **Accademia di Santa Cecilia** (⌧ Concert hall and box office: Via della Conciliazione 4, ☎ 06/6880–1044), the **Accademia Filarmonica Romana** (⌧ Teatro Olimpico, Via Gentile da Fabriano 17, ☎ 06/320–1752), the **Istituzione Universitaria dei Concerti** (⌧ San Leone Magno auditorium, Via Bolzano 38, ☎ 06/361–0051), and the **RAI** Italian Radio-TV series at Foro Italico (☎ 06/368–65625). There is also the internationally respected **Gonfalone** series, which concentrates on Baroque music (⌧ Via del Gonfalone 32, ☎ 06/687–5952). The **Associazione Musicale Romana** (☎ 06/656–8441) and **Il Tempietto** (☎ 06/481–4800) organize music festivals and concerts throughout the year. There are also many small concert groups. Many concerts are free, including all those performed in Catholic churches, where a special ruling permits only concerts of religious music. Look for posters outside churches announcing free concerts. The Church of Sant'Ignazio often hosts concerts in its spectacular nave setting.

Rock, pop, and jazz concerts are frequent, especially in summer, although even performances by big-name stars may not be well advertised. Tickets for these performances are usually handled by **Orbis** (⊠ Piazza Esquilino 37, ☎ 06/474–4776) and the **Ricordi** music store (⊠ Via del Corso 506, ☎ 06/361–2331; ⊠ Viale Giulio Cesare 88, ☎ 06/372–0216).

Dance

The **Rome Opera Ballet** gives regular performances at the Teatro dell' Opera (☞ Opera, *below*), often with leading international guest stars. Rome is regularly visited by classical ballet companies from Russia, the United States, and Europe; performances are at the Teatro dell'Opera, Teatro Olimpico, or at one of the open-air venues in summer. Small classical and modern dance companies from Italy and abroad give performances in various places; check concert listings for information.

Film

Rome has dozens of movie houses, but the only one to show exclusively English-language films is the **Pasquino** (⊠ Vicolo del Piede off Piazza Santa Maria in Trastevere, ☎ 06/580–3622). Films here are not dubbed, but are shown in English, sometimes with Italian subtitles. Several movie theaters show films in the original language on certain days of the week; the listings in *Romac'è* are reliable. Pick up a weekly schedule at the theater or consult the daily papers.

Opera

The opera season runs from November to May, and performances are staged in the **Teatro dell'Opera** (⊠ Piazza Beniamino Gigli, ☎ 06/481–7003). Tickets go on sale two days before a performance, and the box office is open 10–5. Prices range from 26,000 to 142,000 lire for regular performances; they can go much higher for an opening night or an appearance by an internationally acclaimed guest singer. Standards may not always measure up to those set by Milan's fabled La Scala, but, despite strikes and shortages of funds, most performances are respectable.

The summer opera season has been evicted from the ruins of the ancient **Baths of Caracalla.** By 1997, however, a new open-air venue should be ready, probably in Villa Pepoli, a parklike area adjacent to the ruins of the Baths.

NIGHTLIFE

Although Rome is not one of the world's most exciting cities for nightlife (despite the popular image of the city as the birthplace of *La Dolce Vita*), discos, live-music spots, and quiet late-night bars have proliferated in recent years. This has been true in the streets of the old city and in far-flung parts of town. The "flavor of the month" factor works here, too, and many places fade into oblivion after a brief moment of popularity. The best sources for an up-to-date list of late-night spots are the "Night Scene" section of *Romac'è* and *Metropolitan,* an English-language biweekly sold at many newsstands.

Bars

Rome has a range of bars offering drinks and background music. Jacket and tie are in order in the elegant **Blue Bar** of the Hostaria dell'Orso (✉ Via dei Soldati 25, ☎ 06/686–4250) and in **Le Bar** of the Grand hotel (✉ Via Vittorio Emanuele Orlando 3, ☎ 06/482931). **Jazz Club** (✉ Via Zanardelli 12, ☎ 06/686–1990), near Piazza Navona, is a classic watering hole with seating at the bar or in leather-upholstered booths. Light meals are available, and there's live music a few nights a week. It's open from 9:30 PM to 2:30 AM and on Sunday from noon to 4 for brunch. **Flann O'Brien** (✉ Via Napoli 29, ☎ 06/448–0418) has the look and atmosphere of an upscale Irish pub, but it is open all day, also functioning as an Italian coffee bar.

Attendance at **Antico Caffè della Pace** (✉ Via della Pace 3, ☎ 06/686–1216), near Piazza Navona, ranges from coffeehouse intellectuals to showier types. **Bar del Fico** (✉ Piazza del Fico 26, ☎ 06/686–5205), is a down-to-earth, authentically Roman alternative to the more sophisticated bars in the Piazza Navona area. **Le Cornacchie** (✉ Piazza Rondanini 53, ☎ 06/686–4485), near the Pantheon, has an oversize (for Rome) bar, serves meals, and is open until 2 AM.

Beer halls and a plethora of new pubs are popular with young Italians. **Birreria Marconi** (✉ Via di Santa Prassede 9/c, ☎ 06/486636), near Santa Maria Maggiore, is also a pizzeria. It is closed Sunday. **Birreria Santi Apostoli** (✉ Piazza Santi Apostoli 52, ☎ 06/678–8285) is open every day until 2 AM. Among the pubs, **Fiddler's Elbow** (✉ Via dell'Olmata 43, ☎ 06/487–2110) is open 5 PM–midnight and encourages singing. **Four Green Fields** (✉ Via Costantino Morin 42, off Via della Giuliana, ☎ 06/359–5091) features live music and is open daily from 8:30 PM to 2 AM. **Fonclea** (✉ Via Crescenzio 82/a, ☎ 06/689–6302), near Castel Sant'-Angelo, has a pub atmosphere and live music ranging from jazz to Latin American to rhythm-and-blues, depending on who's in town. The kitchen serves Mexican and Italian food.

WINE BARS

Informal wine bars are popular with Romans who like to stay up late but don't dig disco music. Near the Pantheon is **Spiriti** (✉ Via Sant'Eustachio 5, ☎ 06/689–2499), which also serves light lunches at midday and is open until 1:30 AM. **Enoteca Roffi** (✉ Via della Croce 76/a, ☎ 06/679–0896) is near the Spanish Steps. **Cavour 313** (✉ Via Cavour 313, ☎ 06/678–5496), near the Roman Forum, offers snacks and cheese plates to accompany the wine of your choice. **Trimani Wine Bar,** between Piazza della Repubblica and Porta Pia (✉ Via Cernaia 37/b, ☎ 06/446–9630), is the family-run annex of one of Rome's most esteemed wine shops. You can sample some great wines at the counter or with a light, fixed-price meal at an upstairs table. The bar is open Monday–Saturday noon–3:30 and 6–midnight. At **Cul de Sac** (✉ Piazza Pasquino 73, ☎ 06/688–01094), near Piazza Navona, you find good wines and snacks in cramped quarters.

Discos and Nightclubs

Most discos open about 10:30 PM and charge an entrance fee of around 30,000–35,000 lire, which may include the first drink. Subsequent drinks cost about 10,000–15,000 lire. Some discos also open on Saturday and Sunday afternoons for patrons under 16.

There's a full range of disco music at **Smile** (✉ Via Schiaparelli 29–30, ☎ 06/322–1251) for the under-30 crowd, which sometimes includes young actors. Special events, such as beauty pageants, fashion shows, and theme parties, are featured. It is closed from Sunday to Tuesday. An annex is around the corner. **Tatum** (✉ Via Luciani 52) has deafening disco music for the underage. The club is open Thursday–Saturday.

Jackie O' (✉ Via Boncompagni 11, ☎ 06/488–5754) is an upscale favorite with the rich and famous for dinner and/or disco dancing. Roman yuppies mingle with a trendy and sophisticated crowd while dancing to disco music at **Spago** (⊠ Via di Monte Testaccio, ☎ 06/ 574–4999). The club is hard to find, so take a taxi.

Gilda (⊠ Via Mario dei Fiori 97, near Piazza di Spagna, ☎ 06/678–4838) is the place to spot famous Italian actors and politicians. This hot nightspot has a piano bar, as well as a restaurant, dance floors, and live music. Jackets are required. It's closed Monday. **Palladium** (⊠ Piazza B. Romano 8, Ostiense district, ☎ 06/511–0203) is out of the way but has the excitement of innovation in rock, rap, and funky music, whether live or recorded. Closing day varies. The **New Open Gate** (⊠ Via San Nicola da Tolentino 4, ☎ 06/482–4464) has changed mood and is now the trendiest disco in town.

One of Rome's first discos, **The Piper** (⊠ Via Tagliamento 9, ☎ 06/ 841–4459) keeps up with the times and is still a magnet for energetic young adults. It has disco music, live groups, and pop videos. Occasionally, there's ballroom dancing for an older crowd, and Sunday afternoons is for teenagers. It is open from 10 PM until 5 AM and is closed Monday and Tuesday. **Gossip Café** (⊠ Via Romagnosi 11, ☎ 06/361–1348) is a disco where sophisticated under-25s let loose. **Follia** (⊠ Via Ovidio 17, ☎ 06/683–08435) attracts celebrities and a sophisticated young crowd with disco music and a piano bar.

Music Clubs

Jazz, folk, pop, and Latin music clubs are flourishing in Rome, particularly in the picturesque Trastevere and Testaccio neighborhoods. Jazz clubs are especially popular, and talented local groups may be joined by visiting musicians from other countries. As admission, many clubs require that you buy a membership card for about 10,000–20,000 lire.

In the Trionfale district near the Vatican, **Alexanderplatz** (⊠ Via Ostia 9, ☎ 06/372–9398) has both a bar and a restaurant, and features nightly live programs of jazz and blues played by Italian and foreign musicians. For the best live music, including jazz, blues, rhythm and blues, African, and rock, go to **Big Mama** (⊠ Vicolo San Francesco a Ripa 18, ☎ 06/ 581–2551). There is also a bar and snack food.

In case you want to see the world.

At American Express, we're here to make your journey a smooth one. So we have over 1,700 travel service locations in over 120 countries ready to help. What else would you expect from the world's largest travel agency?

do more

AMERICAN
EXPRESS

http://www.americanexpress.com/travel

Travel

In case you want to be welcomed there.

We're here to see that you're always welcomed at establishments everywhere. That's why millions of people carry the American Express® Card – for peace of mind, confidence, and security, around the world or just around the corner.

do more®

AMERICAN EXPRESS

Cards

In case you're running low.

We're here to help with more than 118,000 Express Cash locations around the world. In order to enroll, just call American Express before you start your vacation.

do more

And just in case.

We're here with American Express® Travelers Cheques and Cheques *for Two*.® They're the safest way to carry money on your vacation and the surest way to get a refund, practically anywhere, anytime.
Another way we help you...

do more

AMERICAN
EXPRESS

**Travelers
Cheques**

Latin rhythms are the specialty at **El Charango** (⊠ Via di Sant'Onofrio 28, ☏ 06/687–9908), near Ponte Amedeo d'Aosta, a live music club.

In the trendy Testaccio neighborhood, **Caffè Latino** (⊠ Via di Monte Testaccio 96, ☏ 06/574–4020) attracts a thirtysomething crowd with concerts (mainly jazz) in one room and a separate video room and bar for socializing. **Music Inn** (⊠ Largo dei Fiorentini 3, ☏ 06/688–02220) is Rome's top jazz club and features some of the biggest names on the international scene. It also has a restaurant, which is closed Monday.

Live performances of jazz, soul, and funk by leading musicians draw celebrities to **St. Louis Music City** (⊠ Via del Cardello 13/a, ☏ 06/474–5076). There is also a restaurant. The club is closed Sunday.

For Singles

Locals and foreigners of all nations and ages gather at Rome's cafés on **Piazza della Rotonda** in front of the Pantheon and in the vicinity of **Piazza Navona,** or in **Piazza Santa Maria in Trastevere,** as well as at the host of English, Scottish and Irish pubs that have opened throughout the city. The cafés on **Via Veneto** and the bars of the big hotels draw mainly tourists and are good places to meet other travelers in the over-30 age group. In fair weather, those under 30 will find crowds of contemporaries on the **Spanish Steps,** where it's easy to strike up a conversation.

6 Outdoor Activities and Sports

Beaches

The beaches nearest Rome are at **Ostia,** a busy urban center in its own right; **Castelfusano,** nearby; **Fregene,** a villa colony; and **Castelporziano,** a public beach area maintained by the city. At Ostia and Fregene, you pay for changing cabins, cabanas, umbrellas, and such, and for the fact that the sand is kept clean and combed. Some establishments, such as **Kursaal** (✉ Lungomare Catullo 36, at Castelfusano, ☎ 06/562–1303) have swimming pools, strongly recommended as alternatives to the notoriously polluted waters of this part of the Mediterranean. You can reach Ostia by train from Ostiense Station; Castelfusano and Castelporziano by bus from Ostia; and Fregene by COTRAL bus from Via Lepanto stop of Metro A in Rome. All beaches are crowded during July and August.

For cleaner water and more of a resort atmosphere, you have to go farther afield. To the north of Rome, **Santa Marinella** and **Santa Severa** offer shoals, sand, and attractive surroundings. To the south, **Sabaudia** is known for miles of sandy beaches, **San Felice Circeo** is a classy resort, and **Sperlonga** is a picturesque old town flanked by beaches and pretty coves.

Participant Sports

Biking

You can rent a bike at **I Bike Rome** (✉ Underground parking lot at Villa Borghese, ☎ 06/322–5240) and at **St. Peter Motor Rent** (✉ Via di Porta Castello 43, ☎ 06/687–5714; ✉ Piazza Navona 69). There are rental concessions at the Piazza di Spagna and Piazza del Popolo metro stops, at Largo San Silvestro, Largo Argentina, Viale della Pineta in Villa Borghese, and at Viale del Bambino on the Pincio.

Pedaling through Villa Borghese, along the Tiber, and through the center of the city when traffic is light is a pleasant way to see the sights, but remember: Rome is hilly. **Secret Walks** (✉ Viale Medaglie d'Oro 127, 00136 Rome, ☎ 06/397–28728) organizes all-day bike tours of Rome covering major sights and some hidden ones; summer tours include a stop for a swim. The same tours are available by moped.

Bowling

There's a large American-style bowling center, **Bowling Brunswick** (⊠ Lungotevere Acqua Acetosa, ☎ 06/808–6147), and a smaller one, **Bowling Roma** (⊠ Viale Regina Margherita 181, ☎ 06/855–1184).

Fitness Facilities

The **Cavalieri Hilton** (⊠ Via Cadlolo 101, ☎ 06/35091) has a jogging path on its grounds as well as an outdoor pool, two clay tennis courts, an exercise area, a sauna, and a steam room. The **Sheraton Roma** (⊠ Viale del Pattinaggio, ☎ 06/5453) has a heated outdoor pool, a tennis court, two squash courts, and a sauna, but no gym. The **Sheraton Golf** (⊠ Viale Parco de' Medici 22, ☎ 06/659788) has a fitness center and golf course. The **St. Peter's Holiday Inn** (⊠ Via Aurelia Antica 415, ☎ 06/6642) has two tennis courts on the hotel grounds. It also has a 75-foot outdoor pool.

The **Roman Sport Center** (⊠ Via del Galoppatoio 33, ☎ 06/320–1667) is a full-fledged sports center occupying vast premises next to the underground parking lot in Villa Borghese; it has two swimming pools, a gym, aerobic workout areas, squash courts, and saunas. It is affiliated with the **American Health Club** (⊠ Largo Somalia 60, ☎ 06/862–12411).

Golf

The oldest and most prestigious golf club in Rome is the **Circolo del Golf Roma** (⊠ Via Acqua Santa 3, ☎ 06/784–3079). The newest are the **Golf Club Parco de' Medici** course (⊠ Viale Parco de' Medici 22, ☎ 06/655–3477) and the **Country Club Castel Gandolfo** (⊠ Via Santo Spirito 13, Castel Gandolfo, ☎ 06/931–2301). The **Golf Club Fioranello** (⊠ Viale della Repubblica, ☎ 06/713–8212) is at Santa Maria delle Mole, off Via Appia Antica. There is an 18-hole course at the **Olgiata Golf Club** (⊠ Largo Olgiata 15, Via Cassia, ☎ 06/3088–9141). Nonmembers are welcome in these clubs but must show the membership cards of their home golf or country clubs. Additional information can be provided by **Federazione Italiana Golf** (⊠ Viale Tiziano 74, 00196 Rome, ☎ 06/36851).

Horseback Riding

There are several riding clubs in Rome. The most central is the **Associazione Sportiva Villa Borghese** (⊠ Via del Galoppatoio 23, ☎ 06/ 360–6797). You can also ride at the **Società Ippica Romana** (⊠ Via Monti della Farnesina 18, ☎ 06/324–0592) and at the **Circolo Ippico Olgiata** (⊠ Largo Olgiata 15, ☎ 06/3088–8792), outside the city on Via Cassia. For information on equestrian excursions, contact the **Associazione Nazionale per il Turismo Equestre** (⊠ Via A. Borelli 5, 00161 Rome, ☎ 06/444–1179).

Jogging

The best bet for jogging in the inner city is the **Villa Borghese,** which offers a circuit of the Pincio, among the marble statuary, running about ⅔ kilometers (½ mile). A longer run in the park itself might include a loop around **Piazza di Siena**, a grass horse track. Although most traffic is barred from Villa Borghese, government and police cars sometimes speed through. Be careful to stick to the sides of the roads. For a long run away from all traffic, try **Villa Ada** and **Villa Doria Pamphili** on the Janiculum. On the other hand, if you really love history, jog at the old **Circus Maximus,** or along Via delle Terme di Caracalla, which is flanked by a park (☞ Cavalieri Hilton *in* Fitness Facilities, *above*).

Swimming

The outdoor pools of the **Cavalieri Hilton** (⊠ Via Cadlolo 101, ☎ 06/ 35091) and the **Hotel Aldovrandi** (⊠ Via Ulisse Aldovrandi 15, ☎ 06/ 322–3993) are lush summer oases open to nonguests. The **Roman Sport Center** (⊠ Via del Galoppatoio 33, ☎ 06/320–1667) has two swimming pools, and there's another one at the **American Health Club** (⊠ Largo Somalia 60, ☎ 06/862–12411).

Tennis

Increasingly popular with Italians, tennis is played in private clubs and on many public courts that can be rented by the hour. Your hotel *portiere* (concierge) will direct you to the nearest courts and can book for you. A prestigious Roman club is the **Tennis Club Parioli** (⊠ Largo de Morpurgo 2, Via Salaria, ☎ 06/862–00882).

Spectator Sports

Basketball

Basketball continues to grow in popularity in Italy, with many American pros now playing on Italian teams. In

Rome, games are played at the **Palazzo dello Sport** in the EUR district (✉ Piazzale dello Sport, ☎ 06/592–5107).

Horse Racing

There's flat racing at the lovely century-old **Capannelle** track (✉ Via Appia Nuova 1255, ☎ 06/718–3143), frequented by a chic crowd on big race days. The trotters meet at the **Tor di Valle** track (✉ Via del Mare, ☎ 06/529–0269).

Horseback Riding

The **International Riding Show,** held in May, draws a stylish crowd to the amphitheater of Piazza di Siena in Villa Borghese. The competition is stiff, and the program features a cavalry charge staged by the dashing mounted corps of the carabinieri. For information, call the **Italian Federation of Equestrian Sports** (✉ Viale Tiziano 74, ☎ 06/3685–8528).

Soccer

Italy's favorite spectator sport, *Calcio,* stirs passionate enthusiasm among partisans. Games are usually held on Sunday afternoon throughout the fall–spring season. Two teams—Roma and Lazio—play their home games in the Olympic Stadium at **Foro Italico.** Tickets are on sale at the box office before the games; your hotel portiere may be able to help you get tickets in advance. The Olympic Stadium is on Viale dei Gladiatori, in the extensive Foro Italico sports complex built by Mussolini on the banks of the Tiber (☎ 06/333–6316). For further information, contact the **Federazione Italiana Giuoco Calcio** (✉ Via Gregorio Allegri 14, 00198 Rome, ☎ 06/84911).

Tennis

A major international Grand-Prix tournament is held at the Tennis Stadium at **Foro Italico** in May. For information, call the **Italian Tennis Federation** (✉ Viale Tiziano 70, ☎ 06/368–58510).

7 Shopping

HOPPING IN ROME is part of the fun, no matter what your budget. You're sure to find something that suits your fancy *and* your pocketbook, but don't expect to get bargains on Italian brands, such as Benetton, that are exported to the United States; prices are about the same on both sides of the Atlantic.

Shops are open from 9 or 9:30 to 1 and from 3:30 or 4 to 7 or 7:30. There's a tendency in Rome for shops in central districts to stay open all day, and hours are generally becoming more flexible throughout the city. Department stores and centrally located UPIM and Standa stores are open all day. Remember that most stores are closed Sunday, though this is changing, too. Generally, with the exception of food and technical-supply stores, most stores also close on Monday mornings from September to June and Saturday afternoons in July and August. Most Italian sizes are not uniform, so always try on clothing before you buy, or measure gift items. Glove sizes are universal. In any case, remember that Italian stores generally will *not* refund your purchases and that they often cannot exchange goods because of limited stock. *Always* take your purchases with you; having them shipped home from the shop can cause hassles. If circumstances are such that you can't take your goods with you, and if the shop seems reliable about shipping, get a firm written statement of *when* and *how* your purchase will be sent.

Prezzi fissi means that prices are fixed, and it's a waste of time bargaining unless you're buying a sizable quantity of goods or a particularly costly object. Most stores have a fixed-price policy, and most honor a variety of credit cards. They will also accept foreign money at the current exchange rate, give or take a few lire. Ask for a receipt for your purchases; you may need it at customs on your return home. Bargaining is still an art at Porta Portese flea market and is routine when purchasing anything from a street vendor.

It's possible to obtain a refund on the VAT tax, which is included in the selling price. To be eligible, you must spend at least 300,000 lire in one store. For more information, *see* Smart Travel Tips.

Bargains

You can often find good buys in knitwear and silk scarves at stands on the fringes of outdoor food markets. These vendors move to another market each day, so finding one is a question of luck. On **Via Cola di Rienzo** there is usually a stand with a range of blown-glass items. The market at **Via Sannio** (San Giovanni in Laterano) features job lots of designer shoes and ranks of stalls selling new and used clothing at bargain prices. It is open weekdays 10–1, Saturday 10–6. The morning market in the piazza at the center of the **Testaccio** neighborhood also is known for stands selling designer shoes. For boutique fashions at discount prices, bargain hunters will love **Labels-for-Less** (⊠ Via Viminale 35, in the vicinity of Termini Station), and **Vesti a Stock** (⊠ Via Germanico 170).

Department Stores

Rome has only a handful of department stores. **Rinascente**, near Piazza Colonna, sells clothing and accessories only. Another Rinascente, at Piazza Fiume, has the same stock, plus furniture and housewares. **Coin**, on Piazzale Appio, near San Giovanni in Laterano, has fashions for men and women and housewares. There is another Coin store in the U.S.-style shopping mall at Cinecittà Due (☞ Shopping Malls, *below*). The **UPIM** and **Standa** chains offer low to moderately priced goods. They're the place to go for a pair of slippers, a sweater, a bathing suit, or such to see you through until you get home. In addition, they carry all kinds of toiletries and first-aid needs. Most Standa and UPIM stores have invaluable while-you-wait shoe-repair service counters.

Food and Flea Markets

Rome's biggest and most colorful outdoor food markets are at **Campo dei Fiori** (south of Piazza Navona), **Via Andrea Doria** (about a five-minute walk north of the entrance to the Vatican museums), and **Piazza Vittorio** (down Via Carlo Alberto from the church of Santa Maria Maggiore). There's a flea market on Sunday morning at **Porta Portese;** it now offers mainly new or secondhand clothing, but there are still a few dealers in old furniture and intriguing junk. Bargaining is the rule here, as are pickpockets; beware. To reach Porta Portese, take Via Ippolito Nievo, off Viale Trastevere.

Rome Shopping

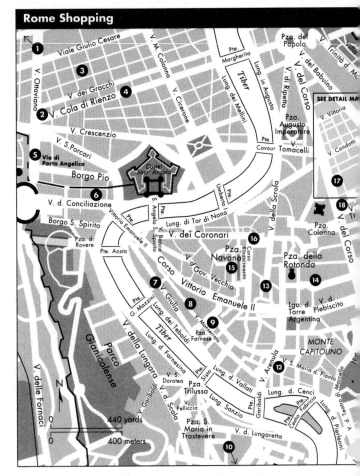

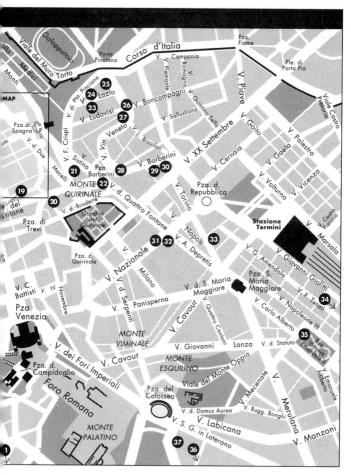

Via Cola di
Rienzo, **4**

Via della
Conciliazione, **6**

Via del
Tritone, **20**

Via di Porta
Angelica, **5**

Via Giulia, **7**

Via Monserrato, **8**

Via Nazionale, **31**

Via Sannio, **37**

Via Veneto, **26**

Volterra, **30**

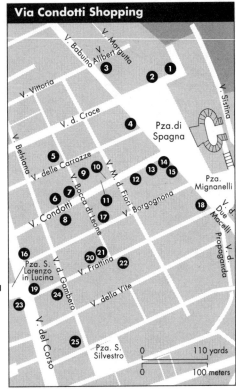

Via Condotti Shopping

All outdoor markets are open from early morning to about 2, except Saturday, when they may stay open all day.

Shopping Districts

The most elegant and expensive shops are concentrated in the **Piazza di Spagna** area especially along **Via Condotti** and **Via Borgognona**. **Via Margutta** is known for art galleries. **Via del Babuino** is the place to go for antiques. There are several high-fashion designer establishments on **Via Gregoriana** and **Via Sistina**. Bordering this top-price shopping district is **Via del Corso**, which—along with **Via Frattina** and **Via del Gambero**—is lined with shops and boutiques of all kinds where prices and goods are competitive.

Via del Tritone, leading up from Piazza Colonna off Via del Corso, has some medium-priced, and a few expensive, shops selling everything from fashion fabrics to trendy furniture. On **Via Veneto** you'll find more high-priced boutiques and shoe stores, as well as newsstands selling English-language newspapers, magazines, and paperback books. **Via Nazionale** features shoe stores, moderately priced boutiques, and shops selling men's and women's fashions. **Via Cola di Rienzo** offers high-quality goods of all types; it's a good alternative to the Piazza di Spagna area.

In Old Rome, **Via dei Coronari** has antiques and designer home accessories. **Via Giulia** and **Via Monserrato** also feature antiques dealers galore, plus a few art galleries. In the **Pantheon** area there are many shops selling liturgical objects and vestments. But the place to go for religious souvenirs is, obviously, the area around St. Peter's, especially **Via della Conciliazione** and **Via di Porta Angelica.**

Shopping Malls

The **Cinecittà Due** mall was the first of several megamalls now catering to Roman consumers, and it is the handiest—just take Metro A to the Subaugusta stop. The mall has 100 shops, including a **Coin** department store branch, a big supermarket, snack bars, and cafés (⊠ Piazza di Cinecittà, Viale Palmiro Togliatti, ☎ 06/722–0902).

Specialty Stores

ANTIQUES AND PRINTS

For old prints and antiques, the **Tanca** shop (⊠ Salita dei Crescenzi 10, near Pantheon) is a good hunting ground. Early photographs of Rome and views of Italy from the archives of **Alinari** (⊠ Via Aliberti 16/a) make interesting souvenirs. **Nardecchia** (⊠ Piazza Navona 25) is reliable for prints. Stands in Piazza della Fontanella Borghese sell prints and old books.

CLOTHING BOUTIQUES

All the big names in Italian fashion—Versace, Ferre, Valentino, Armani, Missoni—are represented in the Piazza di Spagna area. **Sorelle Fontane** (⊠ Salita San Sebastianello 6), one of the first houses to put Italy on the fashion map, has a large boutique with an extensive line of ready-to-wear clothing and accessories. **Carlo Palazzi** (⊠ Via Borgognona

7) has elegant men's fashions and accessories. **Mariselaine** (⊠ Via Condotti 70) is a top-quality women's fashion boutique. **Le Tartarughe** (⊠ Via Piè di Marmo 17) has understated, versatile, and easy-to-wear fashions, including packable knits and jerseys. **Camomilla** (⊠ Piazza di Spagna 85) has trendy styles for women.

HANDICRAFTS

For pottery, handwoven textiles, and other handicrafts, **Myricae** (⊠ Via Frattina 36; ⊠ Piazza del Parlamento 38) has a good selection. **La Galleria** (⊠ Via della Pelliccia 29) in Trastevere is off the beaten track but well worth a visit; it has a wealth of handicrafts, beautifully displayed in a rustic setting. A bottle of liqueur, jar of marmalade, or bar of chocolate handmade by Cistercian monks in several monasteries in Italy makes an unusual gift to take home; they are all for sale at **Ai Monasteri** (⊠ Piazza Cinque Lune 2).

HOUSEHOLD LINENS AND EMBROIDERY

Frette (⊠ Piazza di Spagna 11) is a Roman institution for fabulous trousseaux. **Cesari** (⊠ Via Babuino 195) is another; it also has less-expensive gift items, such as aprons, beach towels, and place mats. **Lavori Artigianali Femminili** (⊠ Via Capo le Case 6) offers exquisitely embroidered household linens, infants' and children's clothing, and blouses. **Jesurum** (⊠ Via Barberini 23) has a good stock of embroidered linens and fine lace.

JEWELRY

Bulgari (⊠ Via Condotti 10) is to Rome what Cartier is to Paris; the shop's elegant display windows hint at what's beyond the guard at the door. **Buccellati** (⊠ Via Condotti 31) is a tradition-rich Florentine jewelry house famous for its silver work; it ranks with Bulgari for quality and reliability. **Fornari** (⊠ Via Frattina 71) and **Frugoni** (⊠ Via Arenula 83) have tempting selections of small silver objects. **Bozart** (⊠ Via Bocca di Leone 4) features dazzling costume jewelry geared to the latest fashions.

KNITWEAR

Luisa Spagnoli (⊠ Via Frattina 116; ⊠ Via Veneto 130) is always reliable for good quality at the right price and styles to suit American tastes. **Miranda** (⊠ Via Bocca di Leone 28) is a treasure trove of warm jackets, skirts, and shawls, handwoven in gorgeous colors of wool or mohair, or in lighter yarns for summer. **Albertina** (⌧ Via Lazio 20) elevates knitwear to the level of high fashion, imparting line and substance to creations that never go out of style.

LEATHER GOODS

Gucci (⌧ Via Condotti 8 and 77) is the most famous of Rome's leather shops. It has a full assortment of accessories on the first floor; a fashion boutique for men and women and a scarf department on the second floor; and many Japanese customers, who line up to get in on busy days. **Roland's** (⌧ Piazza di Spagna 74) has an extensive stock of good-quality leather fashions and accessories, as well as stylish casual wear in wool and silk. **Ceresa** (⌧ Via del Tritone 118) has more reasonably priced fine-leather goods, including many handbags and leather fashions. **Volterra** (⌧ Via Barberini 102) is well stocked and offers a wide selection of handbags at moderate prices. **Sermoneta** (⌧ Piazza di Spagna 61) shows a varied range of gloves in its windows, and there are many more inside. **Di Cori,** a few steps away, also has a good selection of gloves; there's another Di Cori store at Via Nazionale 183. **Merola** (⌧ Via del Corso 143) carries a line of expensive top-quality gloves and scarves.

Nickol's (⌧ Via Barberini 21) is in the moderate price range and is one of the few stores in Rome that stocks shoes in American widths. **Ferragamo** (⌧ Via Condotti 73) is one of Rome's best stores for fine shoes and leather accessories, and its silk scarves are splendid; you pay for quality here, but you can get great buys during the periodic sales. **Mario Valentino** (⌧ Via Frattina 58) is a top name for stylish shoes and leather fashions. In the dolce vita days, Hollywood stars bought their shoes at **Albanesi** (⌧ Via Lazio 21), still a center of fashion in footwear. **Magli** (⌧ Via del Gambero 1; ⌧ Via Veneto 70) is known for well-made shoes and matching handbags at high to moderate prices. **Campanile** (⌧ Via Condotti 58) has four floors of shoes in the latest, as well as classic, styles, and other leather goods.

SILKS AND FABRICS

Galtrucco (⌧ Via del Tritone 18) and **Meconi** (⌧ Via Cola di Rienzo 305) have the best selections of world-famous Italian silks and fashion fabrics. You can find some real bargains when *scampoli* (remnants) are on sale.

8 Excursions from Rome

OSTIA ANTICA

One of the easiest excursions from the capital takes you 7½ miles west to the sea, where tall pines stand among the well-preserved ruins of Ostia Antica, the main port of ancient Rome. Founded around the 4th century BC, Ostia Antica conveys the same impression as Pompeii, but on a smaller scale and in a prettier, parklike setting. It makes for a fascinating visit and a welcome change from museums and churches. Fair weather and good walking shoes are requisites. On hot days, be there when the gates open, or go late in the afternoon.

A visit to the excavations takes two to three hours, including 15–20 minutes for the museum.

Numbers in the margin correspond to points of interest on the Rome Environs map.

❶ **Ostia Antica** was inhabited by a cosmopolitan population of rich businessmen, wily merchants, sailors, and slaves. The great *horrea* (warehouses) were built in the 2nd century AD to handle huge shipments of grain from Africa; the *insulae* (forerunners of the modern apartment building) provided housing for the growing population. Under the combined assaults of the barbarians and the anopheles mosquito, and after the Tiber changed course, the port was eventually abandoned. Tidal mud and windblown sand covered the city, which lay buried until the beginning of this century. Now it has been extensively excavated and is well maintained. **Porta Romana,** one of the city's three gates, opens onto the **Decumanus Maximus,** the main thoroughfare crossing the city from end to end.

Black-and-white mosaic pavements representing Neptune and Amphitrite decorate the **Terme di Nettuno** (Baths of Neptune). Directly behind the baths is the barracks of the fire department, which played an important role in a town with warehouses full of valuable goods and foodstuffs.

On one side of the Decumanus Maximus is the beautiful **theater,** built by Augustus and completely restored by Septimius Severus in the 2nd century AD. In the vast Piazzale delle Corporazioni, where trade organizations similar to guilds had their offices, is the **Temple of Ceres:** This is ap-

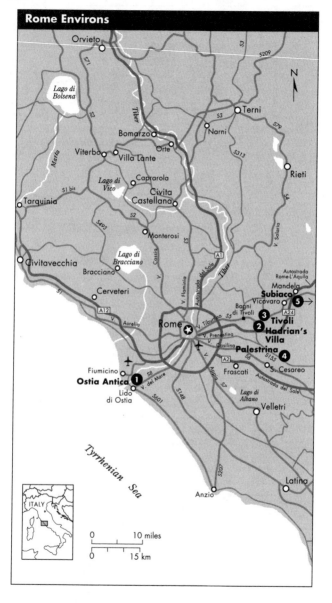

Rome Environs

propriate for a town dealing in grain imports, since Ceres, who gave her name to cereal, was the goddess of agriculture. You can visit the **House of Apuleius,** built in Pompeiian style—containing fewer windows than, and built lower than those in Ostia. Next to it is the **Mithraeum,** with balconies and a hall decorated with symbols of the cult of Mithras. This men-only religion, imported from Persia, was especially popular with legionnaires.

On Via dei Molini you can see a mill, where grain for the warehouses next door was ground with the stones that are still there. Along Via di Diana you come upon a ***thermopolium*** (bar) with a marble counter and a fresco depicting the fruit and foodstuffs that were sold here. At the end of Via dei Dipinti is the **Museo Ostiense,** which displays some of the ancient sculptures and mosaics found among the ruins.

The **Forum** holds the monumental remains of the city's most important temple, dedicated to Jupiter, Juno, and Minerva; other ruins of baths; a basilica (in Roman times a basilica served as a secular hall of justice); and smaller temples.

Via Epagathiana leads toward the Tiber, where there are large warehouses, erected in the 2nd century AD to deal with the enormous amounts of grain imported into Rome during that period, the height of the Empire.

The **House of Cupid and Psyche,** a residential house, was named for a statue found there; you can see what remains of a large pool in an enclosed garden decorated with marble and mosaic motifs. It takes little imagination to notice that even in ancient times a premium was placed on water views: The house faces the shore, which would have been only about ⅓ kilometer (¼ mile) away. Located on Via della Foce are the **House of Serapis,** a 2nd-century multilevel dwelling, and the **Baths of the Seven Wise Men,** named for a fresco found there. There is another apartment building on Cardo degli Aurighi.

The **Porta Marina** leads to what used to be the seashore. In the vicinity are the ruins of the **synagogue,** one of the oldest in the Western world. On Via Semita dei Cippi you can see the **House of Fortuna Annonaria,** the richly decorated house of a wealthy Ostian. This is another place to marvel at the skill of the mosaic artists and, at the same time, to realize that this really was someone's home. One of the rooms opens onto a secluded garden.

The admission charge to the **Ostia Antica** excavations includes entrance to the Ostiense Museum, which is on the grounds. ⊠ *Via dei Romagnoli,* ☎ *06/565–0022.* 🖃 *8,000 lire.* ☉ *Excavations daily 9 AM–1 hr before sunset, museum daily 9–1:30.*

Dining

$$ ✕ **Monumento.** Handily located near the entrance to the excavations, this attractive trattoria serves Roman specialties and seafood. ⊠ *Piazza Umberto I,* ☎ *06/565–0021. AE, DC, MC, V. Closed Mon. and Aug. 20–Sept. 7.*

$$ ✕ **Sbarco di Enea.** Also near the excavations, this restaurant is heavy on ancient-Roman atmosphere, with Pompeiian-style frescoes and chariots in the garden. On summer evenings you dine outdoors by torchlight, served by waiters in Roman costume. You'll probably come for lunch, when you can enjoy *farfalle con granchio* (bow-tie pasta with crab sauce) or linguine with lobster sauce and other seafood specialties, without all the hoopla. ⊠ *Via dei Romagnoli 675,* ☎ *06/565–0034. AE, MC. Closed Mon. and Feb.*

Arriving and Departing

Car

If you decide to go by car, follow Via del Mare, which leads directly from Rome Ostia (a 30- to 40-minute trip).

Train

There is regular train service to the Ostia Antica station from Ostiense train station, near Porta San Paolo; the ride takes about 30 minutes. A long walkway links Ostiense station with the Piramide stop on Metro B; save steps by making connections with the train from Ostiense at the Magliana stop on Metro B. Trains from Ostiense run every half hour. For train information, call 06/4775, 7 AM–10:30 PM.

TIVOLI, PALESTRINA, AND SUBIACO

East of Rome lie some of the region's star attractions, which could be combined along a route that loops through the hills where ancient Romans built their summer resorts. The biggest attraction is Tivoli, which could be seen on a half-day excursion from Rome. But if you continue eastward to Palestrina, you can see a vast sanctuary famous in ancient times. And you could also fit in a visit to the site on which St. Benedict founded the hermitage that gave rise to Western monasticism. The monastery of St. Benedict is in Subiaco—not easy to get to unless you have a car, but you may want to make the effort to gain an insight into medieval mysticism.

This itinerary takes you to two of the Rome area's most attractive sights: Hadrian's Villa and the Villa d'Este in Tivoli, though the road east from Rome to Tivoli passes through some unattractive industrial areas and burgeoning suburbs. You'll know you're close when you see vast quarries of travertine marble and smell the sulphurous vapors of the little spa, Bagni di Tivoli. The Villa d'Este is a popular destination; fewer people go to Hadrian's Villa. Both are outdoor sights, sights that entail a lot of walking, and in the case of the Villa D'Este, stair climbing. That also means that good weather is a virtual prerequisite for enjoying the itinerary.

Hadrian's Villa is about 3 kilometers (2 miles) below Tivoli. Visit Hadrian's Villa first, especially in summer, to take advantage of the cool of the morning. The visit can take from 90 minutes to three hours. The visit to Villa d'Este takes about an hour. (*See* Tivoli, Palestrina, and Subiaco Essential Information, *below,* for how to get to all of the sites from Rome.)

❷ **Hadrian's Villa** was an emperor's theme park, an exclusive retreat where the marvels of the classical world were reproduced for a ruler's pleasure. Hadrian, who succeeded Trajan as emperor in AD 117, was a man of genius and intellectual curiosity. Fascinated by the accomplishments of the Hellenistic world, he decided to re-create it for his own enjoyment by building this villa over a vast tract of land below the ancient settlement of Tibur. From AD 118 to 130, architects, laborers, and artists worked on the villa, periodically spurred on by the emperor himself, as he returned from another voyage full of ideas for even more daring constructions. After his death in AD 138, the fortunes of his villa declined. It was sacked by barbarians and Romans alike; by the Renaissance, many of his statues and decorations had ended up in the Villa d'Este. Still, it is an impressive complex.

The exhibits in the visitors' center at the entrance and the scale model in the building adjacent to the bar will increase your enjoyment of the villa by helping you make sense out of what can otherwise be a maze of ruins. It's not the single elements, but the peaceful and harmonious effect of the whole, that makes Hadrian's Villa such a treat. Oleanders, pines, and cypresses growing among the ruins heighten the visual impact. ⊠ *Villa Adriana.* ▩ *8,000 lire.* ☉ *Daily 9 AM–90 min before sunset.*

NEED A BREAK?   The **Adriano** restaurant, at the entrance to Hadrian's Villa, is a handy place to have lunch and to rest before heading up the hill to the Villa d'Este. The food is good, the cost moderate, and the atmosphere relaxing. It's closed Monday.

---

❸ **Villa d'Este** is the main attraction in the town of **Tivoli.** Ippolito d'Este was an active figure in the political intrigues of mid-16th-century Italy. He was also a cardinal, thanks to his grandfather, Alexander VI, the infamous Borgia pope. To console himself at a time when he saw his political star in decline, Ippolito tore down part of a Franciscan monastery that occupied the site he had chosen for his villa. Then the determined prelate diverted the Aniene River into a channel to run under the town and provide water for the Villa d'Este's fountains. Big, small, noisy, quiet, rushing, and running, the fountains create a late-Renaissance playground. Though time is beginning to take its toll, and the fountains and gardens aren't as well kept as in the cardinal's day, it is easy to see why many travelers of the past considered Villa d'Este one of the most beautiful spots in Italy. ⊠ *Villa d'Este, Tivoli.* ▩ *5,000 lire.* ☉ *Daily 9 AM–90 min before sunset.*

Only 27 kilometers (17 miles) south of Tivoli on S636 and 37 kilometers (23 miles) outside Rome along Via Prenestina, **Palestrina** is set on the slopes of Mt. Ginestro, from which it commands a sweeping view of the green plain and distant mountains. It is surprisingly little known outside Italy, except to students of ancient history and music lovers. Its most famous native son, Giovanni Pierluigi da Palestrina, born here in 1525, was the renowned composer of 105 masses, as well as madrigals, magnificats, and motets. But the town was celebrated long before the composer's lifetime.

Ancient Praeneste, modern Palestrina, was founded much earlier than Rome. It was the site of the Temple of Fortuna Primigenia, which dates from the beginning of the 2nd century BC. This was one of the biggest, richest, and most frequented temple complexes in all antiquity. People came from far and wide to consult its famous oracle, yet in modern times, no one had any idea of the extent of the complex until World War II bombings exposed ancient foundations that stretched way out into the plain below the town. It has since become clear that the temple area was larger than the town of Palestrina is today. Now you can make out the four superimposed terraces that formed the main part of the temple; they were built up on great arches and were linked by broad flights of stairs. The whole town sits on top of what was once the main part of the temple.

Large arches and terraces scale the hillside up to the **Palazzo Barberini,** built in the 17th century along the semicircular lines of the original temple. It's now a museum containing material found on the site, some dating back to the 4th century BC. The collection of splendid engraved bronze urns was plundered by thieves in 1991, but they couldn't carry off the chief attraction, a 1st-century-BC mosaic representing the Nile in flood. This delightful work—a large-scale composition in which form, color, and innumerable details captivate the eye—is alone worth the trip to Palestrina. But there's more: a model of the temple as it was in ancient times, which will help you appreciate the immensity of the original construction. ⊠ *Museo Nazionale Archeologico, Palazzo Barberini, Palestrina,* ☎ *06/953–8100.* 🎟 *6,000 lire.* ☉ *spring and fall, Tues.–Sun. 9–6; summer, Tues.–Sun. 9–7:30; winter, Tues.–Sun. 9–4.*

If you are driving or if you don't mind setting out on a round-about route by local bus, you could continue on to **Subi-aco,** tucked away in the mountains above Tivoli and Palestrina. Take S155 east for about 40 kilometers (25 miles) before turning left onto S411 for the remaining 25 kilometers (15 miles) to Subiaco. Its inaccessibility was undoubtedly a point in its favor for St. Benedict. This excursion is best made by car because it's nearly a 3-kilometer (2-mile) walk from Subiaco to Santa Scolastica, and another half hour by footpath up to San Benedetto. If you don't have a car, inquire in Subiaco about a local bus to get you at least part of the way.

What draws travelers to Subiaco is the 6th-century **monastery of St. Benedict,** a landmark of Western monasticism. Located between the town and St. Benedict's hermitage on the mountainside is the **convent of Santa Scolastica,** the only one of the hermitages founded by St. Benedict to have survived the Lombard invasion of Italy in the 9th century. It has three cloisters; the oldest dates from the 13th century. The library, which is not open to visitors, contains some precious volumes; this was the site of the first print shop in Italy, set up in 1474. ▨ *Free.* ☯ *Daily 9–12:30 and 4–7.*

The monastery of St. Benedict was built over the grotto where the saint lived and meditated. Clinging to the cliff on nine great arches, it has resisted the assaults of humans for almost 800 years. Over the little wooden veranda at the entrance a Latin inscription augurs PEACE TO THOSE WHO ENTER. Every inch of the upper church is covered with frescoes by Umbrian and Sienese artists of the 14th century. In front of the main altar, a stairway leads down to the lower church, carved out of the rock, with yet another stairway down to the grotto where Benedict lived as a hermit for three years. The frescoes here are even earlier than those above; look for the portrait of St. Francis of Assisi, painted from life in 1210, in the Chapel of St. Gregory, and for the oldest fresco in the monastery, in the Shepherd's Grotto. ▨ *Free.* ☯ *Daily 9–12:30 and 3–6.*

In the town of Subiaco, the 14th-century **church of San Francesco** is decorated with frescoes by Il Sodoma. Ring the bell for admission.

Dining

Palestrina

$$ ✕ **Stella Coccia.** In this dining room of a small, centrally lo-
★ cated hotel in Palestrina's public garden, you'll find simple
decor, a cordial welcome, local dishes, such as light and freshly
made fettuccine served with a choice of sauces, and more
unusual items, such as pasta e fagioli *con frutti di mare* (with
shellfish). ⊠ *Hotel Stella, Piazzale Liberazione,* ☎ *06/953–
8172. AE, DC, MC, V.*

Subiaco

$ ✕ **Belvedere.** This small hotel on the road between the town
and the monasteries is equipped to serve crowds of skiers
from the slopes of nearby Mt. Livata, as well as pilgrims
on their way to St. Benedict's hermitage. The atmosphere
is homey and cordial. Specialties include homemade fet-
tuccine with a tasty ragù sauce and grilled meats and
sausages. ⊠ *Via dei Monasteri 33,* ☎ *0774/85531. Reser-
vations not accepted. No credit cards.*

$ ✕ **Mariuccia.** This modern barnlike restaurant, close to the
monasteries, caters to wedding parties and other groups but
is calm enough on weekdays. There's a large garden and a
good view from the picture windows. House specialties are
homemade fettuccine with porcini mushrooms and *scaloppe
al* tartufo (truffled veal scallops). In the summer you dine out-
doors under bright umbrellas. ⊠ *Via Sublacense,* ☎ *0774/
84851. No credit cards. Closed Mon. and Nov.*

Tivoli

$ ✕ **Del Falcone.** A central location—on the main street lead-
ing off Largo Garibaldi—means that this restaurant is pop-
ular and often crowded. In the ample and rustic dining
rooms, you can try homemade fettuccine and cannelloni.
Country-style grilled meats are excellent. ⊠ *Via Trevio
34,* ☎ *0774/22358. No credit cards. Closed Mon.*

Arriving and Departing

By Car

For Tivoli, take Via Tiburtina or the Rome–L'Aquila au-
tostrada (A24). From Tivoli to Palestrina, follow signs for
Via Prenestina and Palestrina. To get to Palestrina directly

from Rome, take either Via Prenestina or Via Casilina or take the Autostrada del Sole (A2) to the San Cesareo exit and follow signs for Palestrina; this trip takes about one hour. To get to Subiaco from either Tivoli or Palestrina or directly from Rome, take the autostrada for L'Aquila (A24) to the Vicovaro–Mandela exit, then follow the local road to Subiaco; from Rome, the ride takes about one hour.

By Bus

COTRAL buses leave for Tivoli every 15 minutes from the terminal at the Rebibbia stop on Metro B, but not all take the route that passes near Hadrian's Villa. Inquire which bus passes closest to Villa Adriana and tell the driver to let you off there. The ride takes about 60 minutes. For Palestrina, take the COTRAL bus from the Anagnina stop on Metro A. There is local bus service between Tivoli and Palestrina, but check schedules locally. From Rome to Subiaco, take the COTRAL bus from the Rebibbia stop on Metro B; buses leave every 40 minutes and those that take the autostrada make the trip in 70 minutes, as opposed to one hour and 45 minutes by another route.

By Train

The FS train from Termini Station to Palestrina takes about 40 minutes; you can then board a bus from the train station to the center of town. For train information, call 06/4775, 7 AM–10:30 PM.

Guided Tours

American Express (☎ 06/67641) and **CIT** (☎ 06/47941) have half-day excursions to Villa d'Este in Tivoli. **Appian Line** (☎ 06/488–4151) and **Carrani Tours** (☎ 06/482–4194) have morning tours that include Hadrian's Villa.

Visitor Information

Tivoli (✉ Largo Garibaldi, ☎ 0774/21249). **Subiaco** (✉ Via Cadorna 59, ☎ 0774/822013).

INDEX

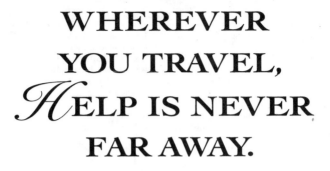

WHEREVER YOU TRAVEL, *H*ELP IS NEVER FAR AWAY.

From planning your trip to providing travel assistance along the way, American Express® Travel Service Offices are always there to help.

Rome

American Express Travel Service
Piazza Di Spagna 38
Rome
6/676-41

Travel

http://www.americanexpress.com/travel

American Express Travel Service Offices are found in central locations throughout Italy.